THE ISLAND
WHISKY TRAIL

AN ILLUSTRATED GUIDE TO
THE HEBRIDEAN DISTILLERIES

NEIL WILSON

ANGELS' SHARE

CONTENTS

First published by

The Angels' Share is an imprint of
Neil Wilson Publishing
303 The Pentagon Centre,
36 Washington Street
Glasgow
G3 8AZ
Tel: 0141 221 1117
Fax: 0141 221 5363
E-mail: info@nwp.co.uk
www.angelshare.co.uk

© Neil Wilson, 2003

The author asserts his moral right under
the Copyright, Design and Patents Act, 1988
to be identified as the Author of this Work.

A catalogue record for this book is available
from the British Library.

ISBN 1-903238-49-8

Printed in Ireland by ColourBooks Ltd
Cover design/typeset by Belstane
All maps by Rob and Rhoda Burns, Drawing Attention
Illustrations on pages 122-3 by Doreen Shaw

The Jean de la Lune *heads up the Sound of Mull to Tobermory*

ACKNOWLEDGEMENTS

IN COMMENCING an adventure such as this, the people with whom I became involved in all sorts of ways build up at a staggering rate. In 1985, the first edition of *Scotch and Water* listed a who's who of the whisky industry along with West Coast worthies, fellow writers and locals from Islay, Jura, Mull and Skye. Today, the list is just as extensive but in revisiting the original theme of the book, I have been fortunate to have been given a great deal of help from Diageo and Dr Nicholas Morgan in particular. His office has been a source of invaluable help, fantastically managed by Lucy Pritchard and the rest of the Classic Malts team including Elaine Bailey and Estelle Rourke who are central in maintaining a sense of order during the Classic Malts Cruise!

The island distilleries are great ambassadors for Scottish hospitality and I owe thanks to all the staff at every Hebridean distillery for their time and efforts on my behalf. Thanks also to the crew of the *Jean de la Lune*: skipper John Reid, his wife Jemma, along with Keith, Bill and Sue and fellow scribe Chris Marais and the Diageo South African contingent of Gerhard Smit and Shirley Swart.

Along the way I have received a considerable amount of help with illustrations and primary research. Graham Fraser of Stirling, an amateur whisky historian who contacted me over two years ago, had been researching the lost distilleries of Islay, an area I had barely touched upon in *Scotch and Water*. With his help I have been able to pull together more information on these concerns and I am indebted to Graham's professional research and the availability of his picture archive. Murdo Macdonald, archivist at the Argyll and Bute District Archives remains much as he was when I first contacted him some 20 years ago … a first-class source of information, a fine fellow and someone who is always able to put his head round the door and mutter, 'This just might be of interest … ' as another revealing source is brought to light. Angus Martin of Campbeltown has revealed so much of the domestic patterns of life and work in the rural communities of Kintyre in the 18th and 19th centuries and the published work of Ian Macdonald of Clachan and Lochgilphead and Dr IA Glen has been invaluable. Alwyn Edgar shed much new light on Hugh MacAskill of Talisker who was responsible for some of the clearances in Bracadale, Skye. His forthcoming 12-volume work on the Clearances is sure to create a huge amount of interest in the subject.

Frank Bigwood's series *The Argyll Courts* has been a godsend as these meticulous records have been culled from the county court records in the keeping of the National Archives of Scotland. Available in searchable CD-rom format, they are an essential requirement for anyone looking for information on Argyll between 1684 and the late 19th century. Contact WFL Bigwood, The Lodge, 2 East Road, North Berwick EH39 4HN (e-mail: wflbigwood@aol.com).

Christine Spreiter, the resident photographer on the Classic Malts Cruise, has allowed me access to all of the images she has captured over the last four years. I am grateful to her for the use of her fabulous pictures.

Rob and Rhoda Burns have produced clear and

Marine Society artist tutor Lincoln Rowe and yours truly tailing a halyard on the Alystra, Sound of Jura, 1984.

concise maps up to their usual standard and the provision of full colour process has helped these tremendously. (robrhoda.graphic@ndirect.co.uk)

Christine Jones and her staff at the Diageo Archive in Menstrie are light years ahead of what used to pass as the company's archives in the early 1980s. Dr Nicholas Morgan deserves especial credit for having had the foresight to bring together the archival material of the former UDV spirits brands and those of Grand Metropolitan under one roof. Now, if you have a genuine research interest in whisky, a pre-arranged visit to Menstrie is all that is required to look over the vast amount of catalogued and filed resource dealing with almost every aspect of the Scotch whisky industry in the last 100 years.

As always my thanks are due to the Ramsays of Kildalton and in particular to the late Mrs Freda Ramsay who managed to maintain many of her grandfather-in-law's papers pertaining to distilling and estate matters on Islay. Without Freda's help and generosity, this book and its predecessor, *Scotch and Water*, would never have happened.

Above all it is always a pleasure to travel to the islands off Scotland's West Coast and revel in their unique atmosphere. As I write this in the third week of March 2003 looking out over the Clyde in Glasgow, with weeks of fair weather behind and the promise of more to come, I can feel the call of the islands drawing me back. To each and every one of the islanders who I have met and worked with over the years, I thank you and envy you your special place in the world.

Neil Wilson

Laphroaig stillhouse reflections

INTRODUCTION

OVER THE LAST 20 YEARS the popularity of single malt Scotch whisky has advanced at a rate that has far exceeded every other category in the Scotch whisky trade. Part and parcel of that appeal has been the fact that single malt Scotch whisky is the product of one distillery – in essence malt whisky distilleries are to the whisky world what the bodega is to Spanish sherry and the chateau to French wine. A single malt is a premier cru – the product of its own special locality and the people who craft it.

This quality is what first drew me to the Hebrides of Scotland in the early 1980s when I searched out the island drams, their histories and the people who made them. I chartered the 38ft steel ketch *Alystra*, skippered by Tony Gill and ably assisted by his wife Anya. Our haven was Ardfern, Argyll, deep in the Celtic homeland of Dalriada and our plan was to sail to Islay, then north to Jura and Tobermory before heading up to Skye.

Some of the people who helped me then have sadly passed on but many of them still remain in the islands, living nearby the distilleries that were once part of their everyday lives. In reality, it is difficult to 'retire' from the whisky business, especially if you are at the coal face as opposed to the retail end of the sector. People like Grant Carmichael who I first met when he was manager at Caol Ila in 1984 is now retired on Islay because he couldn't drag himself away from the place and Iain Henderson of Laphroaig has recently moved to Fife … but is now working at Edradour after one of the shortest-lived retirements on record! Can Iain totally divorce himself from the distillery with which

he has become so inextricably linked? (He worked wonders at Bladnoch and held the helm at Glenlivet for a while.)

The cruise of the *Alystra* to the Hebridean distilleries was published as *Scotch and Water* in 1985 and has been in print ever since. But that journey was not solely about whisky. It was also to do with the sea and the 'water' in the title referred to that. It is the sea that has governed the economy and social patterns of the Hebrides for centuries and this influence has only abated recently with the advent of the roll on/roll off ferries in the 1970s and the demise of the once ubiquitous puffer at around the same time. The Victorians never saw the sea as an obstacle in the way that the politicians and transport gurus of today do. They saw it as an opportunity. In the late 1890s it was possible to leave Rothesay in Bute and travel to the centre of Glasgow faster than it can be done today (unless you have access to a helicopter).

For some years I have wanted to return to the story of the Hebridean malts to bring it up to date. I have looked further into the role of illicit distilling in the islands and Kintyre and have been able to understand the social and commercial role of women in the making of whisky in the late 18th and early 19th centuries in Argyll. This latter element alone flies in the face of the stereotypical perception of how whisky was made outside the law in rural and urban Scotland all those years ago. I was tempted to look more closely at Arran and Campbeltown and their respective roles but there is probably another book required to cover these places in their own right. I have scraped the surface with

The Jean de la Lune.

Campbeltown and will need to revisit this in the future. So as a way of compromise I have looked at the role of distilling in Oban while still concentrating on the areas originally covered in *Scotch and Water*, namely, Islay, Jura, Mull and Skye.

In the late 1980s the world of Scotch whisky changed overnight with the takeover of DCL by Guinness and one wondered what the impact would be on the rest of the industry. Was amalgamation the way forward? If I had concerns then, they were genuine and I feared for the prospects of the likes of Ardbeg, Tobermory and indeed Bruichladdich, as it was gradually sidelined by its owners Invergordon, then Whyte & Mackay and finally Jim Beam Brands (Greater Europe) plc. This book shows that despite the overwhelming market forces that created the Guinness/DCL combine, followed by the emergence of Diageo and the recent dissipation of the assets of the Chivas empire, it was the smaller distillers and independent bottlers who reacted in the boldest manner and stepped in to take over the endangered distilleries.

Effectively this book covers the geographical areas that the Classic Malts Cruise sails through every year on its triangular journey from Oban, down to Islay, then north by Jura and any safe haven in between to Tobermory and finally to Talisker. For anyone wanting an introduction to the Hebrides and its whisky, I suggest they try and make this trip. It is infinitely simpler than doing it yourself as I did in 1984. The CMC can be contacted via World Cruising Club, 120 High Street, Cowes, Isle of Wight, PO31 7AX.

email: classicmaltscruise@worldcruising.com

Tel +44 (0) 1983 296060

Fax +44 (0) 1983 295959.

In order to reprise my original trip, I was privileged to be a crew member on Scotland's only square rigger, the *Jean de la Lune*, during the Classic Malts Cruise of July 2001 as we made our way from Caol Ila to Skye during a spell of glorious West Coast weather. What made the trip special was the fact that many overseas journalists were experiencing this part of the world for the first time and I was able to indulge myself in their sense of awe in what they were experiencing. As a Scot, it made me very proud of the natural assets in which my country abounds.

The Island Whisky Trail is exactly what it says it is. I hope that in here you will find a feast of information on the distilleries, their creators (and illicit forebears), the islands themselves and, hopefully, this will encourage you to go out and try the drams (if you have not done so already!). In 1984 only one home-trade bottling of single malt was available from Ardbeg, Lagavulin, Laphroaig, Bruichladdich, Bowmore, Bunnahabhain and Talisker. Tobermory was struggling with a vatted malt called Ledaig, Port Ellen was well nigh unobtainable and Caol Ila was only dispensed by Grant in his wonderful office above the Sound of Islay. (Believe me, there is no finer office location in the world.) Now I am worried that if I list the Hebridean bottlings available as we go to press, it will be out of date before the ink is dry. If you are ever in dire need of a Hebridean bottling, look no further than Richard Joynson's excellent Loch Fyne Whiskies (www.lfw.co.uk) as Richard stocks just about everything on the planet.

In 1984 a visitor to Ardbeg had to contact head office and correspond with the manager (or rather caretaker-manager) to arrange a visit. Take a look at the place now. That is what makes this journey so fulfilling. Once it looked as though we were going to lose places like Ardbeg and Bruichladdich forever, but now we can journey into their souls as they resonate to the fascinating rhythms of the music of whisky making.

It is from this simple, unpretentious industry that today's Hebrideans are taking the art and craft of the old island distillers to the rest of the world in the 21st century.

Slàinte Mha!

The Kildalton Cross, Islay

CHAPTER ONE

A BARBAROUS PEOPLE

THIS ISLAND hath a liberty of brewing whisky ... ' wrote the Reverend Archibald Robertson in 1793 in his Parish report for Kildalton, Islay, in the *Old Statistical Account of Scotland*. His observation was no exaggeration, and arouses as much curiosity in the amateur historian as it does in any visitor to the island. On studying a modern-day map of the Inner Hebrides the question arises, 'Why so many distilleries on Islay?', for there are eight in all, and to the east there is one at Lochranza on Arran, another on Jura just to the north, one on Mull, and another on Skye. Apart from Lochranza which was established a decade ago, the others are the remnants of a once ubiquitous industry that covered almost the entire Highland and Islands of Scotland. And even as I write plans are in process to construct a traditional farm distillery at Kilchoman on Islay. What were the main factors in this evolutionary process?

At first glance, all these distilleries appear to be unusual places in which to establish commercial concerns, in remote and unlikely settings, some distance from the mainland and with no easy means of access. But their origins can be hinted at with the unwitting help of some of the great scholars, academics and travellers of the past few centuries who made the Hebrides a subject of their letters and books and gave us many insights into the lives and customs of the islanders.

These chroniclers are now part of established Hebridean literature, among them Martin Martin, Thomas Pennant, Sam Johnson, John Knox, the Reverend James Macdonald, Alfred Barnard, John MacCulloch, Hugh Miller, Joseph Mitchell and the great Lowland distiller John Ramsay. Many ministers of the Church of Scotland recorded their observations in the Parish reports which formed those most remarkable commentaries on society, the Old and New Statistical Accounts of 1794 and 1844.

Islay, as the most southerly of the Hebridean islands, lies within 17 miles (27.2 km) of the coast of Ireland, and as early as the 6th century the Scots had crossed into Argyll from Ireland and established the new territory of Dalriada. In AD 678, they clashed in battle with the Britons on Jura and in AD 719, two Dalriad tribes opposed each other on Gigha. Having firmly established themselves and uniting with the Picts around AD 843, the Scots gradually gave their name to the new nation which largely adopted their Celtic form of speech.

Some 600 years later the art of distillation is believed to have been carried over the same water to Islay, an island eminently well suited to its execution with unlimited supplies of peat, burns running brim-full with soft water and a fertile soil for that most vital ingredient, grain. The intervening years had brought the Hebrides under the rule of the Norwegian crown which, after the unsuccessful expedition of King Haco in 1263 to maintain sovereignty, finally ceded the islands three years later to King Alexander III of Scotland. By that time, however, they were Norwegian in name alone, for their control had been effectively destroyed in the 12th century by Somerled, from whom the Lords of the Isles were descended. One of Somerled's grandsons, Donald,

The Marquess of Huntly would have become one of Scotland's most famous mass-murderers had he not incurred the wrath of the Presbyterians on King James' Privy Council in the early 17th century

started the great house of Macdonald which assumed the Lordship until 1493 when, through their recklessness and rebellion, they forfeited both the title and their lands to the Scottish crown.

However, the Macdonalds' dominion had never been firmly established, for the islands were habitually in the hands of several clans, all of them powerful and some of them none too well disposed to each other. The MacLeans of Duart on Mull were in possession of lands granted them by John Macdonald, Lord of the Isles, in 1366 through the marriage of his daughter to Lachlan Lubanach MacLean of Duart. Other MacLean factions held between them much of Mull, Tiree, Jura, Scarba, Lochaber, Coll and Rum. The two families of MacLeod held Lewis and Harris whilst sharing Skye and Raasay. Similarly the MacNeils were

two independent families living on Barra and Gigha, while the Macdonalds held Islay, the seat of the Lord of the Isles.

Over the course of the 16th century these clans literally lived in their own world, oblivious to the sovereignty of the Scottish Crown, warring amongst themselves, exacting their own forms of justice and frequently settling arguments with the sword. Raiding was common and profitable; MacLean of Duart plundered Gigha in 1579, returning to Mull with no less than 500 head of cattle and 2,000 sheep and goats. A long-standing feud with the Macdonalds was finally settled in 1598 at Gruinart, Islay, the MacLeans returning to Duart with their tails firmly between their legs.

Distilling was by then an established practice in the islands, the product being a coarse brew, drawn from local cereals such as oats. A hefty draught of this aquavitae would have given an eager warrior greater heart in those troubled times and probably hospitalised an ordinary mortal today. When the fighting eventually subsided, King James VI demanded that MacLean and Macdonald come to Edinburgh to discuss the future of the Isles. Unwittingly, they walked into a trap and were imprisoned in Edinburgh Castle where they naturally begged for mercy. Surprisingly, the king let them off on condition that they simply behave themselves. A few years later they returned to the James's favour when they agreed to contribute more to the treasury by increasing the amount due for the rent of their lands, which Macdonald, of course, had had to pay since the forfeiture of 1493.

Not for the first time the king's warnings went unheeded as the Hebrides remained lawless, harbouring criminals and smugglers alike. The Stewart succession to the English throne complicated James' efforts to find a solution when the Royal Court was removed to London in March 1603. He believed adamantly in the Union of Crowns and of a united Britain, desiring 'a perfect Union of Laws and Persons, and such a Naturalising as may make one body of both Kingdoms under me your King …' In relentless pursuit of this ideal he decided to finally rid himself of the rebellious inhabitants of the Isles and in 1607, totally exasperated, he agreed to nothing less than the extermination of the entire Hebridean population. This unbelievable proposal, of which many Scots remain ignorant, was to be carried out by the Marquess of Huntly, who was given one year in which to 'extirpate the barbarous people of the Isles …'

But the marquess was a Catholic, and being a powerful man he naturally attracted the attention of the Presbyterian power-players who managed to have him confined by the Privy Council to the Burgh of Elgin and its environs. Fortunately for the islanders, his confinement meant he was unable to carry out his bloody mission, and unfortunately for the marquess he was constantly harangued with sermons from zealous Presbyterian preachers in the hope that he might renounce the Church of Rome.

In 1608 King James again tried to force rebellious chiefs into submission by sending an overpowering fleet under the charge of his Lieutenant, Lord Ochiltree, to intimidate the island strongholds into submission. The fleet took the Macdonald's Dunyveg Castle by Lagavulin in Islay followed by the inland fortress on Loch Gorm before moving quickly north to Mull, where MacLean of Duart, realising the extent of the fleet as it anchored in the Bay of Torosay, surrendered.

Ochiltree then moved up the Sound of Mull to Aros, near Salen, to hold court with the island chiefs. They included Donald MacAllan, Captain of Clanranald, Donald Gorm MacDonald of Sleat, Ruairidh MacLeod of Harris, Hector and Lachlan MacLean of Duart and Angus Macdonald of Dunyveg, who immediately pledged himself once more to the Crown and was allowed to return to Islay forthwith. But Ochiltree remained on his guard and took counsel from the Bishop of the Isles who was present. Together they masterminded a piece of pure theatre for the unsuspecting chiefs. All but MacLeod of Harris (who may have smelt a rat and managed to make his excuses and return home) were invited to hear a sermon from the bishop and then retire to dine aboard Ochiltree's ship, *The Moon*. When assembled there, and doubtless having partaken of much wine, Ochiltree announced, 'Gentlemen, I have the honour as his Majesty's Lieutenant of the Isles, to inform you that you are now his Majesty's prisoners.' And with that, the ship weighed anchor and sailed for Ayr, where the Privy Council despatched the chiefs to a number of scattered castle dungeons until they had learnt their lesson.

But if James thought that he was finally making some headway against the island chiefs, he made sure the point was not lost and pressed home his advantage. In 1609 he appointed the Bishop of the Isles to enact a number of Statutes at Iona (or Icolmkill), outlining proposals deemed necessary by his commission to create a civilised society throughout the Isles. This comprehensive survey of social design presents fascinating insight into the state of life in the Isles in the late 16th and early 17th centuries and gives an understanding of what King James and the Privy Council considered to be the root evils prevalent at the time – needless to say, drink was one of them. Once more the chiefs were assembled to hear the bishop who this time preached far more than a mere sermon.

Bishop Andrew began with a subject dear to his heart, namely the Kirk. The First Statute proposed that those ministers set down in each island parish 'shall be reverently obeyed, their stipends dutifully paid them, the ruinous kirks with reasonable diligence repaired, the Sabbath solemnly kept, and committers of adultery, fornication and incest severely punished.' Handfasting, that is the testing of fertility before a marriage was solemnised, was also declared illegal. Martin Martin explained this in 1703:

It was an ancient custom in the Isles that a man take a maid to his wife, and keep her for the space of a year without marrying her; and if she pleased him all the while, he married her at the end of the year, and legitimized her children; but if he did not love her, he returned her to her parents.

Perfectly straightforward one would think, but James was no fool for outlawing handfasting since he was well aware of what happened in Skye in 1599. That year Donald Gorm handfasted with Margaret MacLeod, the sister of Ruairidh, and bore her away to Duntuilm Castle. Things did not go too well between them and when Margaret injured her eye, Donald Gorm decided he had had enough and sent her back to Dunvegan. Unfortunately he did this in an extremely unsubtle manner, and Margaret arrived back at Dunvegan astride a one-eyed horse, attended by a one-eyed groom and followed by a one-eyed mangy dog. Ruairidh was incensed and all hell broke loose. The ensuing 'War of the One-Eyed Woman' lasted two years, ending in the rout of the MacLeods at Coire na Creiche above Glen Brittle. Thankfully, it did at least signal the end of clan fights in Skye.

The Second Statute had a more profound effect on the landscape for it proposed the establishment of inns and hostelries in convenient places within every isle, selling food and drink at reasonable prices. Many change-houses were built thereafter at junctions and ferry points along the length of the drove roads which carried the island cattle to the mainland markets.

The Third Statute forbade the presence of malingerers who had no means or occupation within the Isles, and limited the number of gentlemen whom each chief could entertain in his household. Macdonald of Dunyveg, Donald Gorm MacDonald, Ruairidh MacLeod, and Donald MacAllan were limited to six, MacLean of Duart to eight and the lesser men, three.

Under the Fourth Statute beggars and sorners who, until then had existed by the ancient right of extracting maintenance from the common folk, were banished unless they could pay for their needs at one of the inns.

The chiefs were probably not too concerned at this point, but the worst was about to come. Bishop Andrew claimed under the Fifth Statute that ' … one of the special causes of the great poverty of the said Isles, and of the great cruelty and inhuman barbarity practised by sundry of the inhabitants of the same upon others their natural friends and neighbours, has been the extraordinary drinking of strong wines and aquavitae brought in amongst them, partly by merchants of the mainland and partly by some traffickers dwelling amongst themselves.' This, the bishop deemed would have to stop, and he proposed that importation of spirits cease, and that anyone found smuggling should pay 40 Scots pounds for the first offence, rising to 100 pounds for the second, with a third and final offence resulting in the forfeiture of all buildings, goods and possessions. But most surprisingly of all, and this demonstrates how great a factor drink was in Hebridean society, the Statute demurred ' … without prejudice always to any person within the said Isles to brew aquavitae and other drink to serve their own houses, and to the said special barons and substantious gentlemen to send to the Lowlands and there to buy wine and aquavitae to serve their own houses.'

The Sixth Statute required that the gentlemen of the Isles send at least their eldest son, or having none, daughter, to school in the Lowlands to learn to 'speak, read and write English.'

The carrying and use of firearms was expressly

forbidden under the Seventh Statute, even for the shooting of game. This must have been greeted with horror by the assembly, who were as attached to their broadswords and muskets as they were to their drink.

Curiously, the Eight Statute banned bards from the Isles. Considering their high social standing as hereditary poets and historians in Hebridean households, this proposal must have been as unpopular as the last.

The Ninth, and final, statute was a catch-all undertaking which bound them all to enforce the entire set of statutes. But how effective were these measures on a people who had previously displayed little respect for the authority of the king? The immediate effect was negligible, as history records that the Macdonalds continued to flout the law. This led to the eventual pacification of Islay by the clan that for years had remained closest to the crown … the Campbells.

By 1614, the Privy Council called on Sir John Campbell of Cawdor (or Calder) to take possession of Islay and subdue the Macdonalds once and for all. He was well placed to do so, being both powerful and rich enough to afford the rental. He took control of the island in 1615, claiming 'the forfeitures of all those in Argyll and Kintyre' and thus began an association between the Campbells and Islay which was to last until 1854.

The remaining chiefs were bound over in Edinburgh the following year to implement the statutes, which were made tougher, if a little more realistic with regard to the carrying of arms. This they could now do, but only in the service of the king, or if hunting within a mile of their homes. However, there was a catch; their homes were to be set down in one place alone, meaning that MacLeod of Harris had to stay at Dunvegan in Skye, MacLean of Duart at Duart Castle in Mull, Clanranald at Eilean Tioram in Moidart,

MacLaine of Lochbuie at Moy Castle in Mull and Gorm of Sleat at Duntuilm in Skye.

Their drinking habits hadn't changed much, and a reduction in their household allowances was implemented. Duart, MacLeod and Gorm were all restricted to four tuns of wine a year, amounting to the not inconsiderable sum of over 1,000 old gallons. If this seems somewhat excessive, Samuel Morewood reminds us in his exquisitely entitled book of 1838, *Inebriating Liquors*, how these quantities were habitually consumed:

In the Western Islands, many of the customs of the ancient Caledons and Britons are still preserved, and amongst others, the old manner of drinking. In former times, large companies assembled, composed principally of the chief respectable men of the islands. This assemblage was called a 'sheate', 'streah' or 'round', from the company always sitting in a circle. The cup bearer handed about the liquor in full goblets or shells, which the guests continued to drink until not a drop remained. This lasted for a day at least, and sometimes for two days, and in this practice our 'round of glasses' is supposed to have originated. During the revel, two men stood at the banqueting door with a barrow, and when anyone became incapable, he was carried to his bed, and they returned to dispose of the others in the same way.

These binges were the only means available to the chiefs of relieving the unremitting gloom of the 17th century; the present-day 'ceilidh' has its roots in these intoxicating gatherings. While wine was most commonly drunk by these 'respectable men', aquavitae (or usquebaugh in Gaelic) remained the drink of the people and as such was produced on a small scale, relying on the availability of grain.

As a result of many seasons of wet weather, for much

of the first half of the 17th century the island inhabitants suffered from low yields of bere, or bigg (the indigenous strain of West Coast barley). Their problems were often compounded by the common practice of paying rents with grain. Until some form of effective agrarian and social reform arrived in the Hebrides, distilling remained a sporadic activity designed to satisfy the needs of the local market. Aquavitae itself became a relatively precious commodity – a glut of grain often meant a burst of distilling activity which created much needed cash. Quite often distilling resulted in a shortage of grain for food, causing more problems than it solved. Islay, being the most naturally fertile island in all the Hebrides, was best placed to benefit from the gradual reforms, which began to produce results in the 18th and 19th centuries.

In the meantime, the major use for the land throughout the Hebrides was for the raising of stock, almost all of which found its way to the London market. The Union of the Crowns in 1603 had created a huge demand for black cattle on the London market and vast herds were moved down from the islands along the drove roads, which, largely due to the Second Statute, were serviced with change-houses. The responsibility for taking charge of cattle, sometimes representing more than half the total value of Scotland's exports to England, never weighed heavily on the minds of the hardy drovers as they slaked their thirsts at these inns. Long established sites of these change-houses can still be seen on either side of the Sound of Islay at Port Askaig and Feolin Ferry, Jura, and further up the 'Long Road' along Jura's east coast at Corran House, Lagg, and in the far north of the island at Kinuachdrach.

In 1644, the Scots Parliament levied the first excise on spirits, largely to bankroll the Royalist army. Whether enough was raised from the 2s 8d on each

'Great' Daniel Campbell of Shawfield who purchased Islay in 1726. The Campbell family's ownership would last until 1853.

Scots pint is debatable, since a great deal of distillation was still well outwith the reach of the law. The turmoil that engulfed mainland Britain during the insensitive reign of Charles I and Cromwell's Protectorate appears to have left the islands largely unaffected. The Campbells consolidated their grasp on Islay and Jura, having imported many kinsmen to act as tacksmen, taking long or indefinite leases or tacks on large grazing farms. They in turn had sub-tenants who, not being responsible for the rent, worked the land for no pay. This system became a considerable financial burden on the family, for only the success of the cattle droves realised the greater part of the rental payments. Poor harvests and unprofitable droves created low farm incomes, rent arrears, and often, more multiple tenancies that were extremely difficult to reverse.

Following the letter of the First Statute of Icolmkill,

the Kirk's ministers had persevered, often ineffectually, within the island parishes. A clandestine Franciscan mission from Ireland between 1612 and 1646 had succeeded in converting some 10,000 Hebrideans, a fact which the Protestant clergy chose to ignore and one which had moved King James to comment ' … anybody who converts so wild a people … to Christianity, even if Catholicism, deserves to be thanked.'

At the end of the 17th century, Martin Martin from Skye travelled through the isles, observing that on Lewis the inhabitants drank:

Several sorts of liquors, as common Usquebaugh, another call'd Trestarig, id est Aquavitae, three times distill'd, which is strong and hot; a third sort is four times distill'd and this by the Natives is call'd Usquebaugh-baul, id est Usquebaugh, which at first taste affects all the Members of the Body: two spoonfuls of this last liquor is a sufficient Dose; and if any Man exceed this, it would presently stop his breath, and endanger his life.

Colonsay, he recorded as still being a Catholic enclave, where the Protestant minister was much resented as a burden dependent on his parishioners, taking solace in drink for 'in the presence of several gentlemen and others, after drinking of aquavitae to excess and the bottle ending sooner than he desyred, chapped on it with his hand and said the devil put the bottom out of it.' The synod took a dim view of this as well, and threw the unfortunate man out of the Kirk.

The century closed badly for the country in general with several years of appalling harvests. Much of the population was on the brink of starvation, unable to pay the rents, which were often raised and commonly in arrears. The Union of Parliaments in 1707 effectively ended Scotland's political autonomy, leaving the future of the Hebrides very much in the hands of the lairds.

Due to the long-standing tenure of the Campbells (and, no doubt strengthened by their reputation of being the king's men), Islay and Jura were exempted from direct control of the Scottish Board of Excise, and the levies remained 'in farm' to the laird. Clearly this was the simplest solution to the problem of policing a remote region, but it was far from being the most efficient.

It was in Islay that the most profound influences on the distilling industry within the Isles would eventually manifest themselves; but their beginnings were to be found in the abominable conditions that prevailed in the early years of the 18th century. In 1717, much of the livestock had perished from cattle plague, having subsisted on the corn and barley that had been put aside for the tenants who were 'next to beggary'. John Campbell, himself financially embarrassed, had just succeeded to an estate which was rapidly running downhill. Accordingly, in 1723 he agreed to a loan of £6,000 (and £500 per annum thereafter for 21 years) from one of Scotland's leading merchant financiers, 'Great' Daniel Campbell of Shawfield, MP for Glasgow Burghs, Deputy Lieutenant of Lanarkshire, and as shrewd and astute a businessman as his namesake was naïve and inept. Shawfield received as security a mortgage on Islay for 21 years or until the money was repaid.

Shawfield's advantage in this deal was furthered by his own misfortune in 1725 when he voted in parliament for an increase of 3d on the tax on a bushel of malt. This infamous Malt Tax was designed to offset a proposed excise duty of 6d on a barrel of ale, and was part of a programme to equalise duties on excisable liquors in Scotland and England, despite the fact that no mention of a tax on malt had been made in the Act of Union.

The Glasgow mob was incensed and vented its anger directly at Campbell, sacking Shawfield mansion in June of 1725. With customary foresight, Campbell had managed to move many valuables in time, but the damage was such that his bill of compensation from the City of Glasgow amounted to £9,000. Within a year Shawfield had managed to turn his lease into a sale of all the Campbell of Cawdor lands in Islay, including part of Jura, for £6,000 over and above the previous settlement. It is commonly believed that the purchase was due to the compensation Shawfield received after the riots.

'Great' Daniel Campbell laid the foundations that changed Islay's agricultural system from one of winter and summer grazings with common pasture to one of larger farms supporting fewer tenants. He was particularly conscious of the fact that employment had to be created for a large number of the tenantry outwith the agricultural sector, giving greater diversity in both jobs and services. Distilling activity appears to have remained around the croft on a small scale because in 1772 only one-eighth of Islay's grain crop was barley, some of which would have been used to make aquavitae. However, this figure tends to confirm Thomas Pennant's observation when he visited Islay in the same year, that 'in old times the distillation was from thyme, mint, anise, and other fragrant herbs, and ale was much in use with them.'

The Malt Tax adversely affected the brewers who adulterated their ale causing a general reduction in consumption. People turned to spirituous liquors which in the Lowlands of Scotland were largely based on cereals other than malted barley, thus avoiding the tax. Home distillers were not liable to pay excise duty, unless supplying the local market, as was probably the case in remote regions like the Hebrides where the face of the Exciseman was rarely, or as in Islay's case, never seen. However, advantage was gradually taken of the greater yield of alcohol from malted barley and dutiable output increased on the mainland. Scottish aquavitae escaped being taxed in the Gin Act of 1736,

which was introduced in an effort to reduce consumption of English Gin and imported Dutch Genever; consumption of aquavitae thus doubled in 1737 to over 200,000 gallons (900,000 litres).

'Great' Daniel died in 1753, the estate passing to his grandson, Daniel the Younger on his coming of age five years later. Around this time aquavitae generally became accepted as a malt-derived drink, while usquebaugh was mainly the type of beverage which Pennant described. Until 1777, Daniel the Younger continued his grandfather's work as a progressive improving laird, overseeing the development of a profitable flax industry and encouraging the mining of copper, silver and lead. Two-rowed barley, as opposed to the four-rowed bere, was grown to increase yields along with other crops such as turnip and clover grass, as more acreage was put to the plough. His most outstanding achievement was the creation of Bowmore in the late 1760s as the new centre of commerce for the island.

As the population of Islay increased dramatically from around 5,300 in 1753 to over 7,000 by the time the new village was constructed, new sources of employment had to be created and Campbell was quick to realise that distilling was one such source. A distillery at Bowmore was rapidly erected by David Simson, who had previously distilled in Bridgend, at the head of Loch Indaal.

Simson set the pattern for many of the commercial island distillers who followed him – all were men of diverse interests, the majority being farmers using their own barley. In this way they enjoyed a security which did not force them to depend on distilling as their sole means of income. However, Islay's position, although improved, was by no means perfect. Even after the considerable exertions of the Shawfield Campbells, it was not far removed from the situation existing throughout the rest of the Hebrides as famine and its incumbent ills were never far away. Pennant saw a great deal which impressed him in Islay but also observed 'people worn down with poverty: their habitations scenes of misery, made of loose stones; without chimnies [sic], without doors excepting the faggot opposed to the wind at one or other of the apertures, permitting the smoke to escape through the other, in order to prevent the pains of suffocation … the inmates, as may be expected, lean, withered, dusky and smoke dried.'

Famine did grip Islay and the entire nation in 1782 and a ban on distilling was made in Argyll in an effort to save grain stocks. The government sought to reduce legal output by nearly doubling duty to 4s per gallon of spirit. Nevertheless, the public's thirst for whisky remained unquenched and dram drinking (a dram being one-third of a pint of whisky containing 60% abv) was now a popular habit, both on the mainland and in the Isles. The product of the stills was of much higher quality than the Lowland grain-based whisky, due to the traditionally small stills and weak washes. The malt whisky produced by the home distillers in the Highlands was smuggled in huge quantities into the Lowlands where it was held in great esteem. The Excise were kept extremely busy dealing with this illegal trade, which had become a thorn in the side of the legal distillers, themselves overburdened by outmoded excise regulations.

In 1874, one of the turning points in the development of the whisky industry within the Isles occurred when the government passed the Wash Act in an attempt to ease the restrictions on the legal trade and encourage illicit distillers to take out a licence. It proved to be unsuccessful, but was amended the following year in such a way as to allow each parish two stills of 30-40 gallons (136-181 litres) volume, operated by respectable tenants appointed by their lairds, and paying a licence of £1 10s per gallon of still volume. Many such licences were taken out, even though only 250 bolls of malt grown in the local parish could be used in each still per annum.

The act also prohibited the export of whisky from the Highlands to safeguard the interests of the large Lowland distilleries. This measure backfired because the Highland product was in such great demand in the Lowlands that smuggling continued unabated, even as the output of legal spirit nearly quadrupled in the space of two years. But most significantly of all, the Wash Act was the beginning of the end of home distillation. Those who made it at all in the accessible Highlands did so in quantities large enough to reap them high returns from the smugglers, while the licensed stills often consumed more that the 250-boll limit which the act decreed – a practice which the Excise often chose to ignore. Only in the far reaches of the Highlands and Islands did the small stills gurgle away unhindered in their bothies, the face of the gauger rarely seen and little cared for.

On Islay, where the gauger would not arrive until 1797, Bowmore Distillery was well established and Duncan Campbell had just left the island after distilling at Ardmore for some time. The new laird, Walter Campbell, following his elder brother who died at the age of 40 in 1777, still faced the continuing problem of a growing population; but he relentlessly pursued his policy of agrarian reform as the Reverend John McLiesh, Minister for Kilchoman parish reported in the *Old Statistical Account*:

The present proprietor has more than doubled his rents; yet the tenantry, as well as himself, are better off than ever. They have given him, as it were, an addition to his estate, by rescuing many acres of moor and moss, from a state of nature, and bring them to yield good crops of corn and grass. On the other hand, the proprietor has given the tenants such advantageous leases, that they have greatly bettered their circumstances as well as increased their numbers, and are enabled to live much more comfortably than formerly.

But distilling had created its own special problems within Islay, as McLiesh's colleague Archibald Robertson concluded in his parish report for Kildalton:

We have not an Excise officer in the whole island. The quantity therefore of whisky made here is very great; and the evil, that follows drinking to excess of this liquor, is very visible in this island. This is one chief cause of our great poverty; for the barley, that should support the family of the poor tenant, is sold to the brewer for 17s the boll; and the same farmer is often obliged to buy meal at 11.3s Sterling, in order to keep his family from starving. When a brewer knows that a poor man is at a loss for money, he advances him a trifle on condition that he makes him sure of his barley at the above price; and it is often bought by the brewers

even at a lower rate; while those who are not obliged to ask for money until they deliver their barley, receive 20s or more for it. This evil, of distilling as much barley as might maintain many families, it is hoped by some means or other, will soon be abolished. It may take some time, however, to prevent the people from drinking to excess; for bad habits are not easily overcome: but there would surely be some hopes of a gradual reformation, if spirituous liquors were not so abundant, and so easily purchased.

Robertson correctly foresaw the coming of the gauger, but underestimated his impact for when the Exciseman did arrive, he was accepted by the legal trade and almost totally ignored by the illicit distillers. By 1800 the situation was so bad on the island that it was suggested troops be sent to support the officers. They never did arrive, for local volunteers had been recruited and persuaded to 'do their duty'. The resources of the Excise were nevertheless stretched,

A lime kiln on the Oa, Islay

and they had particularly bad relations with the McGilvray bothers, Archibald and Alexander, who had been outlawed since 1798 after non-appearance at trial for 'maltreating the Revenue officers'! A 20-guinea reward was offered for information leading to their capture, but to no avail.

The Stent Committee of Islay, which was a latter-day local community council consisting of the laird, his tacksmen and prominent tenants, gave vent to their feelings on the matter in March of 1801, when the minutes of their biannual meeting in Bowmore recorded their resolve to inform on illegal distillers. Perhaps not surprisingly, two of the signatories of this resolve were themselves legal distillers, David Simson of Bowmore and Donald McEachern of Bridgend who were no doubt keen to see precious grain going to the right people – and precious it was, for distilling was banned by the government later that summer following a disastrous harvest. The ban was re-enforced the next year, so it is highly unlikely that much illicit distilling was taking place at all, due to the extreme scarcity of barley in the island.

At this time Tobermory was in the relatively fortunate position of being a busy fisheries port clearing large quantities of goods, grain and liquor while offering a number of services to passing ships. The distillery was again a small affair situated on the harbour front having been established in 1798 by the young merchant John Sinclair who went on to make a considerable fortune in the area. Even with Tobermory's privileged position, its whisky never gained the reputation or commercial success that the other island malts were to enjoy – a fact that the new owners of the distillery are trying hard to rectify.

All the island distilleries supplied local needs at the end of the 18th century, but they were influenced by any legislation that the government was prepared to introduce to control the smuggling of high quality malt

John Ramsay, distiller, Justice of the Peace, Member of Parliament and Laird of Kildalton – 'a man of large intelligence and practical common sense', and one of the most progressive and humanitarian landlords of his time.

from the Highlands into the Lowlands. Increases in duty proved detrimental to the legal distillers in the Highlands and many of them returned to making whisky illegally. The Excise themselves were hindered in the execution of their duties by poor pay and inept laws which made them financially responsible for any volunteers that they might have to use. The measures, which were eventually introduced in the first three decades of the 19th century to eradicate illegal distilling, formed the basis of the present-day industry in the Hebrides.

The lairds held a trump card in the fight against illicit distillation for the threat of eviction was often enough to discourage the practice. In the first year of the 19th century, 157 convictions for illegal distilling occurred on the Duke of Argyll's Tiree estates, with every tenth person being evicted. Walter Campbell's efforts on Islay were not so severe, for the distillers were rarely caught, and the practice continued to occupy the

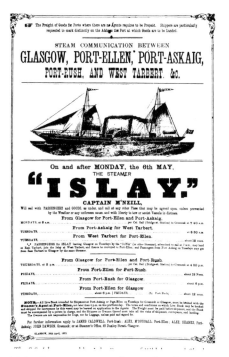

A MacBrayne poster of 1872 for the steamer Islay

Excise officers until at least 1850. In Kintyre the illicit trade reached its heights between 1797 and 1817 when there were no licensed operations and where nearly every glen had several small active stills (see Appendix 4, p136). Most of these were operated by informal companies of men and women who later entered the legal trade. The local Campbeltown plumber, Robert Armour, who also ran a lucrative still making operation, was turning over £350 per annum servicing and supplying the illicit trade during that time.

The legal distillers in the Hebrides were fortunately men of diverse means during the first 15 years of the 19th century, for little production was possible due to a run of poor harvests and wet summers – so severe at times that even the cut peat could not dry properly. At such times, the illicit distillers did not require the attention of the Excise, for their activity must have been greatly reduced. The supply of grain remained the overriding factor in production of malt whisky within the islands until it could be guaranteed by imports (which, until Napoleon's defeat in 1815, were limited). The war with France had led to a severely

depressed economy, which in turn resulted in reduced revenue from spirits.

In 1816, the treasury was persuaded to reduce the level of duty, and thus encourage distillers to 'go legal', helping to increase revenue at the same time. The Small Stills act of the same year allowed the use of stills of 40 gallons (181 litres) minimum volume, even weaker washes, and abolished the 'Highland Line', finally creating a uniform geographical market in which the Highland and Lowland distillers competed equally.

This act dramatically increased the number of distilleries in the Highlands, with a similar burst of legal activity on Islay. New distilleries sprang up at Newton and Octomore while traditional sites of distillation at Lagavulin and Ardbeg were 'invaded' by legal operators. The Jura Distillery, which had started in a similar manner six years before, would have been none the worse for the change in regulations.

Walter Campbell died in 1816 and the estate passed to his grandson, Walter Frederick, who was to be the last Shawfield laird of Islay. He was, unfortunately, a victim of circumstance, but still managed to advance the reforms begun by his predecessors and was generous in granting advantageous leases to his tenants. The financial burdens that he inherited were eventually to be his downfall, even as Islay, and particularly the distilling industry in the island, thrived.

By 1848, another nine operations had started, of which the most famous survivor is Laphroaig. Their success was largely due to the fact that the malt produced was in such great demand on the mainland that the local markets were of a lower priority. Production was now registered in thousands and not hundreds of gallons per year, but the most critical factor in their success was the Excise Act of 1823. This Act was simple but effective, allowing the continuance of small stills, but halving duty to 2s 5d per gallon of spirits produced and sanctioning a drawback of 1s 5d per gallon if the spirit was pure malt whisky, thus offsetting the greater cost of malted barley. A licence fee of £10 was all that was required for a distiller to go legal. It was now possible for legally-produced malt whisky to taste as good, and cost less than the smuggled item. The effect of the legislation in Kintyre was profound as illicit distillers realised that it made commercial sense to begin operating within the law. It was from this point on that Campbeltown was to emerge as Scotland's busiest distilling town.

Whereas the Illicit Distillation (Scotland) Act of 1822 was to have the greatest impact on the mainland, where heavy penalties were introduced, very few convictions were brought in Islay as the distillers were rarely caught in the act – even when the Excise had employed the Customs Cutter SS *Chichester* to make runs along the southern coast of the island. What they gained in speed, they lost in conspicuity.

By 1833, the building of Talisker Distillery had been completed on the remote shore of Loch Harport in the Isle of Skye, increasing the portfolio of island distilleries that survive to this day. The inland distilleries established during Walter Frederick Campbell's lairdship on Islay were all to fail eventually – only those occupying the relatively convenient seashore sites would survive into the next century. Another factor was the immense resource of distilling knowledge that had grown with the illicit trade and held in trust by men and women alike before being absorbed into the legal trade in the early 1800s. Women were pivotal in the development of distilling along the West Coast during this period.

The Islay estate was finally sold to the English merchant James Morrison in 1853 – the descendant of a Scots drover who, after delivering cattle to Wiltshire, married and settled there. By then the industry in the islands was almost wholly subject to the wider economic forces which prevailed throughout the industry on the mainland. Its only peculiarity was this dependence on the sea for transport of goods and produce to and from the mainland and export markets.

It is very likely that many of the island distilleries would not have survived an economic disadvantage such as this were it not for the fact that, of all the distillers in Scotland, only the hardiest and most resilient managed to succeed in the islands, and as we shall see, of all the whiskies, the island malts still most perfectly reflect these qualities.

Derelict farm buildings at Octomore, near Port Charlotte, that were once used for distilling.

CHAPTER TWO

ARGYLL

OBAN DISTILLERY was established in the early 1790s, around the same time as its counterpart in Tobermory, by a family who were to have a profound influence on the development of both of these ports. The Stevensons, who seem to have been an entrepreneurial lot, helped to transform Oban from a coastal village to a busy, prosperous trading and manufacturing community. The brothers John and Hugh were responsible first for creating a shipyard in the town and then in 1793 a brewery, later converting it into a distillery. In Tobermory they built the harbour breastworks but left the distilling business there to the prominent Morvern-based merchant, John Sinclair.

John Stevenson was a builder and construction expert and his father had been a well-known mason in Argyll. John inherited this trade and worked on a number of kirks, bridges and private dwelling houses in Argyll. His other interest lay in the management of a slate mining quarry that was based further down the West Coast at Easdale. Hugh furthered his family's interest in the material by purchasing the slate-rich island of Balnahua in 1780, while also renting the neighbouring Garvellach isles for sheep pasture.

Along with a third brother, Thomas, a fish curer at Bonawe, John and Hugh traded in all sorts of merchandise and goods subject to excise duty. They moved spirits, wines and port along the coast and traded in heavier materials required in construction work and farming. The profits from their trade were ploughed into property in and around Oban and they

were directly responsible for designing and building much of the town on tacks leased from the Duke of Argyll. They then feued more land from the Duke, his tacksmen and the Marquis of Breadalbane. For his efforts, in 1819 Hugh was eventually elected as Oban's second Provost.

Like so many other distillers, their route into the business was through their brewery. In 1793 the two brothers formed, with other business partners, the Oban Brewery Company, and commenced operations on the corner of Stafford Street and George Street on ground that had previously been held as a tack from the Duke of Argyll. A year later the brewery was producing 'cowbell ale' but by the turn of the century Hugh Stevenson & Co, distillers, were in business on the same site. As brewing had been prohibited in 1795-6 throughout Scotland due to a shortage of grain, Stevenson may have sensed that there would be an increased demand for whisky after the prohibition was lifted.

John Stevenson, in his capacity as trustee for the Oban Brewery Company, purchased the distillery in 1804. It then occupied the old brewery itself and the brewery garden to the rear of the site. The seller was the estate of the Haddington banker, Hay Smith, who had been sequestrated following his purchase of the land and the leases from the Duke of Argyll. The distilling company remained in business throughout this period, but records are sketchy as to when activity may have ceased. Certainly the Stevensons were never ones to concentrate on one business venture at a time and Hugh's son, Thomas, had been farming in Argentina for some years before returning from Buenos Aires in 1813. He had amassed a considerable fortune and he gradually began to invest in the area prior to the death of his father in 1820. His uncle John had died some two years earlier. By 1823 he had purchased all the assets of the brewery business from the remaining partners and a year later he took over the distillery proper.

He also fell heir to his father's slate quarries at Balnahua and managed these directly as well as establishing the Caledonian Hotel on land he owned in George Street. Thomas's eldest son, John, assisted him in the distillery after he returned from Argentina sometime after 1822. John was a natural distillery manager and he somewhat eclipsed his father with his natural business acumen.

However, the fortune that Thomas had amassed was being whittled away and he had a reputation for being careless with his money. Thomas's other son, Hugh, remained in South America and wrote to his mother from Peru in 1828 stating that, 'He, you, and myself know that money flies through his fingers God knows how, without doing any good to himself.' Soon the distilling business required capital and Thomas entered into a bizarre arrangement with the Edinburgh printing firm, Duncan Stevenson & Co, whereby each firm accepted the others' bills for discounting. The printing business was jointly owned by Thomas's younger brother, the Campbeltown sheep rancher Capt Hugh Stevenson, and his namesake, Duncan, a printer to trade with a penchant for property development and someone who

was not unfamiliar with bankruptcy.

Inevitably, the printers went bust and Duncan Stevenson was sequestrated, so bringing the distillery business's finances sharply into focus. Thomas kept the wolf from the door by bartering whisky and slate to his major creditors, but in 1829 the axe fell on him too. His son John soldiered on, eventually securing leases for the distillery and its house later that year. By the end of 1830 he had shrewdly bought the business and the distilling plant outright for £1,500 – about half its valuation.

John kept a steady hand on the helm until sometime before 1861 as it is then that his name disappears from the local census records. His family had certainly been residents in George Street along with his brother Hugh, and his son, also Hugh, who had been employed as clerk in the distillery. John's own son, Thomas (born in South America in 1822), and his wife and family were also resident in the same street, but Thomas died in Glasgow in 1860 and this might explain why John's interest in the business waned.

In 1862 the firm of A&R Walker, distillers in Oban, were purchasing malting equipment from Wm McOnie & Co of Glasgow and enlarged the production capacity of the distillery. They sold out in 1866 to the local merchant Peter Cumstie who, along with six other Cumsties' in his family, namely William, Alexander, James, George, Patrick and Arthur, held land and properties directly in front and to the south of the distillery. Peter Cumstie then leased the business to William Gillies of 112 St Vincent Street, Glasgow. Three years later on Saturday, April the 10th, John Stevenson died at Balliemore, on the island of Kerrera, which lies just offshore from Oban. A week later *The Oban Times* ran a fulsome tribute to the old man:

The Late Mr Stevenson
In the death of this much-lamented gentleman, which sad event occurred at Balliemore, Island of Kerrera, on the morning of Saturday last (not Thursday as mentioned in our obituary of last week), another of the ancient landmarks of Oban has been removed. He was, publicly and privately, so very intimately connected with the earlier history of the town that we feel his loss to be, to a considerable extent, a disruption of the

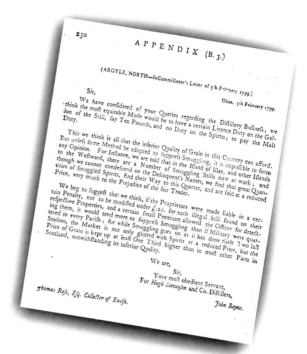

A letter of 1799 to the all-powerful Collector of Excise on behalf of the Oban Distillery pleading for the plight of the 'fair trader'.

sympathies which bound the present to the past. Public spirited, and hospitable to a fault, his name will long be remembered by the inhabitants proper, as a 'household word'. Some facts regarding his antecedents will, we are sure, be read with interest by many of our readers who were acquainted with Mr John and the other members of the Stevenson family.

Three brothers Stevenson, Hugh, John, and James [sic], came from Dumbartonshire, and settled in Oban about 90 years ago. Some years after settling here they commenced shipbuilding; and subsequently they started a brewing and distilling business. At one time they possessed a large part of the house property in Oban. Deceased, Mr John Stevenson, was a grandson of Hugh, one of these brothers. He went to South America when a lad; and after being in business there for some years, he returned home – upwards of 40 years ago. He resided in Oban for upwards of 30 years afterwards. During that time he was proprietor of the Oban Distillery, and was an extensive farmer. He was a public spirited and popular man, and frequently held the office of Chief-Magistrate of the burgh. He was one of the founders of the Oban Curling Club, and an ardent curler. He was a member of the Oban Lodge of Freemasons, and was until lately their Grand Master. About 9 years ago he left Oban, and up to the time of his death resided at Balliemore, in the Island of Kerrera. Deceased was in politics a moderate Liberal; and on several occasions he was, from his influential position and popular character, of great service to the Liberal party in Oban. Deceased was seventy years of age when he died. For the last few years his health was in a very infirm state, and the event which took place last week was not unlooked for for some time previous. His remains were carried from Kerrera last Wednesday and deposited in the Parish Churchyard here. A good number of people from town and country turned out on the occasion to pay a last tribute of respect to their old friend. The procession formed at and marched from the Port Kerrera Ferry to the place of interment, a distance of about two miles. From being a member of the Masonic brotherhood, Mr Stevenson's funeral was

Oban at the turn of the 18th century with the distillery chimney clearly visible at the far end of the harbour.

attended by a large body of the fraternity. At the place of interment the Masonic burial ritual, which is simple and impressive, was used. The address was read by the Rev P McKercher, MA, and the prayers said by the Rev R J Macgeorge, the Chaplains of the Lodge.

Alfred Barnard arrived in Oban on his tour of the distilleries of the United Kingdom in 1886 aboard a steamer and stayed in the Craigard Hotel before making his rounds the next day. He states the year of establishment as 1794 and the then proprietor as a James Walter Higgin who had taken over the concern from William Gillies in 1883. He in turn had succeeded the Walkers in 1878. Barnard recorded that after Higgin had acquired the lease he ' … had also made vast improvements in the machinery and appliances, and built two new Bonded warehouses.'

He then went on to describe the layout of the distillery in some detail.

We first bent our steps to the outer courtyard, on two sides of which, in the form of a triangle, are the Granaries and Malt-barns. They are built with stone, and, being nearly a century old, have a very ancient

appearance. An outside stone staircase gives access to the two upper floors, which are used for storing the barley. The ground floors are concreted, and each possesses a stone Steep. At the end of the building there is a kiln, which is 30 feet square, and is floored with wire cloth. It is heated with peats, enclosed in an old-fashioned brick furnace. The sides of this enclosure are very spacious, and are used for storing and drying the peat; there is besides on the hill, a large shed which contained sufficient for two years' consumption. On a level with the floor of the Kiln and communicating therewith is a Malt Deposit 50 feet long and 27 feet wide, capable of storing 400 quarters of malt. At this place the raw material changes its residence from one side of the quadrangle to the other, and a rustic timber bridge has been thrown across the way, over which the dried malt is wheeled to the basement building containing the malt cylinders and mill machinery, driven by steam. The top flat is used as the Grist Loft, and contains a hopper, into which the pulverized malt is tipped before passing through the Mashing-machine. We next followed our guide through a narrow doorway, and found ourselves on a platform overlooking the Mash House, whereon are placed two antiquated timber Heating Coppers, holding together 2,000 gallons, and a sparger. Descending to the floor, we are shown the Mash-tun, a peculiar little metal vessel standing on the ground; it is 9 feet in diameter and 5-feet deep, containing the usual stirring gear driven by steam. Mr. Gordon here drew our attention to a loft over head, where is placed the Worts Receiver, to which we ascended and obtained a view of the Coolers; they consist of an open shallow tank forming the inside roof of the Tun-room. From this receptacle the worts run by gravitation into the Washbacks. Descending a few steps, we then passed through an archway direct into the Tun Room, a building by itself, bearing indisputable marks of antiquity. It contains seven Washbacks, each holding 1,200 gallons. We next proceeded to the Still House passing under a gallery on which is placed the Wash Charger, which holds 1,200 gallons, and the Worm Tub and Water supply, one of them of singular construction and position. It consists of a narrow timber trough or tank high up in the air, stretching right across the yard, and contains an enclosed pipe, leading direct from the lade through which runs a continuous stream to the worms, and passing out on the other side, the water is utilized to turn the rummager of the Wash Still. We had seen the Still House before from the distiller's parlour, but on entering it from the court, and observing its walls and roof, it presented the appearance of a monastic building. It still contains two old Pot Stills, one a Wash Still holding 1,000 gallons, the other a Spirit Still holding 500 gallons, both heated by fire, and the rummagers therein driven by water from the Worm Tub. There is a platform running across the old building, on which are placed the Low-wines and Feints Charger and Safe, and in the adjoining chamber are the Receivers. Following our guide, we next entered the Spirit Store, which forms the basement of the offices, and was formerly the distiller's kitchen. It contains a Spirit Vat of 1,200 gallons content, and the casking appliances. Opposite there is a small Cooperage and cask shed; and also a 10-horse power engine, which has been at work upwards of forty years, and shows no signs of decay; also a steam boiler, 14 feet long and 5 feet in diameter. Distributed about the premises are four Warehouses; two of them are newly built, and although not of large dimensions, are of great height and solid construction. That most recently finished is three stories high, and measures 60 feet by 30 feet, and will hold 60,000 gallons of Whisky. Lower down the hill there is a second building, also of three stories, 78 feet by 30 feet. These new Warehouses are fitted up with fixed gauntrees on every floor, the timber

The view down Stafford Street which clearly shows the distillery offices that existed before the building of the malting floors.

supports of which are most substantial, and run from the ground to the roof, so that they will bear any weight, and help to support the building; they are arranged so that any cask can be removed without affecting its neighbour. The whole of the Warehouses together will store 3,500 casks.

The Whisky is not only pure Highland Malt, but a good self Whisky, and the annual output is 35,000 gallons.

Unfortunately for Higgin, his investment was fated to suffer a severe setback when a fire engulfed the offices and adjoining still house in May 1890, as *The Oban Times* reported:

Serious Fire at Oban Distillery
Shortly after ten o'clock this morning (Thursday) fire broke out in the low range of buildings in Stafford Street, belonging to the distillery, and used principally as a still-room and offices. The flames spread rapidly, and in the course of half an hour gained complete hold

of the roof and woodwork. Fortunately, there was a plentiful supply of water at hand. The appliances at the distillery for use in such an emergency were at once put into requisition, and under the direction of Mr Higgin, the proprietor, did much to keep the fire from spreading to the adjacent buildings, where a large quantity of whisky was stored. The hose of the fire brigade was somewhat tardy in making its appearance, but once placed in position, a steady stream of water was promptly poured into the burning mass, and in about an hour thereafter, all danger to the surrounding property was considered to be at an end. The fire is said to have arisen from the over-heating or bursting of the still which at the time, contained a quantity of whisky. The damage to the property, though as yet not exactly known, is considerable; and, we understand, Mr Higgin is only partly insured. Large crowds assembled at the scene to witness the progress of the fire, and, in addition to the fire brigade, there were many willing hands, whose services were of much avail. Among the more conspicuous of these might be mentioned Mr Campbell, the burgh surveyor; Mr Neill MacColl, builder; Mr Robertson, gas manager; Mr Archibald MacDougall, son of the late Coll MacDougall, merchant and others. The latter got his hand badly cut, and was attended to by Dr MacCalman. The books and papers in the counting-room were all safely taken out of the building; and Mr Higgin himself displayed great energy during the progress of the fire.

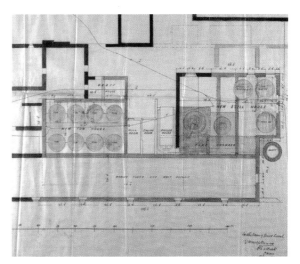

A plan from June 1890 drawn up shortly after the fire.

But was Higgin only partly insured? If the next eight years are anything to go by, it seems not. Within a month of the blaze, plans were produced for a new distillery layout that clearly shows a new still house to the rear of the site adjoining the northern boundary of the Cumstie family's holdings. Further plans are dated 26th June showing new drains and the whole exercise was repeated for a new office building astride Stafford Street in 1894 with further additions in 1898. Either way, Higgin was not skimping on investing in the distillery, or his backers weren't. But whoever or whatever was behind this great outlay of capital, it was eventually to bring Higgins's involvement with Oban to an end. By the time of the last survey another problem was looming ... one that was to have far-reaching effects on the whole of the trade.

It was at precisely this time that one of Oban Distillery's main debtors, Robert Pattison of Pattison, Elder & Company, the Leith merchants and blenders, came to an arrangement with Higgin over the ownership of the business. Pattison was directly involved in the flotation of the Oban & Aultmore-Glenlivet Distillery Co which realised a profit of £40,000. This was largely due to the fact that the subscribers were hell-bent on riding on the back of the late-Victorian whisky boom which was coursing through the trade, manifesting itself in the creation of a number of new malt distilleries. The problem was

that much of this optimism had been created by the Pattison brothers, Robert and Walter, whose credit-worthiness as far back as 1894 had been noted by the board of the Distillers Company as being extremely doubtful. Despite their concerns, they continued trading with the Pattisons as they were simply too important to them.

The problem did not go away. For some years the Pattisons had been sailing too close to the wind and most of the proceeds from the flotation of the Oban & Aultmore-Glenlivet Distillery Co ended up financing the building of Robert's mansion on the banks of the River Tweed at Kingsmeadows, Peebles. In 1899, the contents alone were valued at £19,000.

Despite the fact that the Pattison brothers went bankrupt, the company remained in business until 1923 when it became part of John Dewar & Sons via their newly-formed subsidiary the Oban Distillery Co. Two years after the Dewar takeover it was finally in the DCL fold and was transferred to Scottish Malt Distilleries in 1930. The licence was then transferred to John Hopkins & Co, a company founded in 1874 and absorbed into the DCL in 1916 before being wholly acquired by them in 1931. A period of mothballing followed until 1937 when production was started again. For the next three decades the distillery remained active until the autumn of 1968 when the distillery and maltings were closed (along with North Port in Brechin and Glen Lochy in Fort William) but then reassessed and opened again the next year. The company's new faith in the distillery was made clear when, between Christmas 1971 and June 1972, the stillhouse was upgraded from coal-fired stills to internal steam coil heating.

Work started on the stripping out the malt barns overlooking George Street on 15 May 1989 in order to create a visitor reception centre. This facility was opened on 18 September that year but was only part completed prior to the interpretative floor on the mezzanine being kitted out completely in late 1990. Between 8 January and 24 May 1991 the mashhouse was refurbished and the completed reception centre was opened by HRH The Princess Royal on 30 May, 1991. In February 1993, the cast iron vessels were removed from the stillhouse along with the worm tub

and all were replaced with stainless steel, but the stills remained untouched. At the same time the boiler was isolated from the stillhouse.

The Oban Distillery Bicentenary was marked by a return visit of HRH The Princess Royal on the 18 October 1994 when she was presented with 200 bottles of Oban malt and a cheque for £20,000. Both of these donations were to go towards Save the Children, a charity to which the Princess is closely associated.

The final development before the new millennium saw Skakel and Skakel's new makeover of the visitor centre facilities (which is what the visitor sees today) carried out in between 6 March to 18 July 1998 so bringing Oban fully into the Classic Malts mould. As one of Diageo's six Classic Malts Oban has clearly benefited from the investment that the growth of that brand has created. Visitors to Oban are well-catered for with guided tours of a very high standard. Anyone wanting to visit is advised to book in advance.

The view over the bay from above the distillery.

Oban Distillery

Stafford Street, Oban, Argyll PA34 5NH
Tel: 01631 572004 Fax: 01631 572011
www.malts.com
Owners: Diageo
Manager: Kenny Gray
Site Operations manager: Willie J MacDougall

Oban Distillery is best approached from the sea and it's no surprise that this is where the annual Classic Malts Cruise kicks off each year. The distillery is hemmed into Stafford Street at the foot of a steep cliff that rises to the structure of McCaig's Tower which dominates the town's skyline. The whole place is an example of 'guid gear in sma' bulk', and is one of the most compact distilleries in Scotland. This, however, does not prevent it from hosting the inaugural party in the back yard before the start of every Classic Malts Cruise.

If you are coming by car you can use the park-and-ride on the A85 on the hill as it drop towards the town, in the long-term car park behind Corran Hall further down the brae, by the pier or on any of the metered bays along the front. There are a few spaces directly outside the distillery in Stafford Street. The visitor centre exudes the influence of Skakel & Skakel, the design consultancy responsible for these facilities at many of the Classic Malts distilleries: bright, stylish and engaging.

According to Duncan and Wendy Graham in their essential *Visiting Distilleries* guide book, first published in 2001, the tour is 'in the top echelon'. The beauty of it is that the compactness of the layout of the plant, which has changed remarkably little from the 1890s when Higgin was rebuilding the place, lends itself perfectly to an in-depth, focussed look at how malt whisky is made. Willie J MacDougall showed me round the plant and we fairly hit it off, as we discovered that we shared similarly varied careers before settling on one direction. By the end of my visit, I had even agreed to buy his Honda Africa Twin motorcycle from him for another travel project planned for the summer of 2003!

Outwith the distillery Oban is beginning to evolve and has lost much of the tackiness and dreariness it exuded in the 1980s. A new fish restaurant, *Ee-usk* (Gaelic for fish) seems to exemplify this – good, local food in good measure. And the old pier is gradually being developed in order to draw in the summer yachties and the like. The comparison with Tobermory is clear, and just as Tobe has got to grips with itself, so Oban seems to be following ... just as the Stevensons had once planned.

Illicit Distilling in the County of Argyll

IF OBAN is the modern face of industrial distilling in Scotland, then a close look at the old county of Argyll during the 17th, 18th and 19th centuries reveals the widespread nature of illicit distilling. Records drawn from the processes of the Argyll Courts show that aquavitae, as the precursor to whisky was called, was in ready supply in the late-17th century and as a commodity subject to excise duty, was of more than just a passing interest to the Exciseman. In effect, a large section of the population was actively involved, on a day-to-day basis, with the manufacture and distribution of illicit whisky. And many of these people were women.

It is accepted that by the mid-18th century, aquavitae was becoming a malt-based spirit distilled throughout the country, having evolved from the raw distillate mentioned by Pennant and other early visitors to Scotland at the end of the 18th century. Consequently its value began to increase as it became more popular and of increasing importance as a source of ready cash in the rural communities. This also made it an everyday issue with the Excise. In 1723 the Collector of Excise summoned 124 people to the court in Inveraray on charges of failure to pay duties. Not all of these people were involved in malting, brewing and distilling as the excise also levied duty on other commodities such as candles and leather. Of the total summoned, 14 were found to be dead when the summons was executed and a number of others were abroad or had moved on. The justices ordered those who were distillers, liquor retailers and victuallers to pay the duties and fines but stated their concern at the number of people summoned for failure to pay duty on candles and leather and who they did not believe to be involved in trading these goods.

In February 1727, the local Collector of Excise, Archibald Campbell had the JP court at Inveraray summon Gilbert Monroe, John Mckellar jun, James McAlester, Margaret McLachlan, Donald Campbell and Margaret Strachan (all were distillers except Monroe)

for failure to pay arrears of duties along with nine others for concealment of liquor upon which duty was payable. All were residents of Inveraray. Only two persons – one in each group – were absolved.

Barely one month later Campbell brought another action against 50 people from Lorn (sic) and 24 from Cowal who were summoned for arrears in payment of duties. Again they were either distillers or victuallers. A search of the processes of the JP courts in Inveraray between 1674 and 1825 shows how much of the court's time was taken up in excise matters and how determined many of the local brewers, distillers and other traders were to avoid paying duty.

In January 1730 ten people from the town were summoned for concealing dutiable liquor. One of them, Anne Roy McNiccoll had hid hers in an 'unentered' room (that is one that was not approved by the Excise for the storage of spirits) and barely six months later she was caught at it again after concealing spirits in a peat loft. Her dedication to the trade was not uncommon amongst the womenfolk of Argyll. Perhaps the single most fascinating aspect of these records is the major role that women played in distilling whisky. When Bessie Williamson was running Laphroaig in the 1950s and 60s she was referred to as Scotland's first female distiller. Nothing could have been further from the truth. In 1772, when Pennant was touring the country, he remarked that women made whisky while their men were at work in the field. Further proof lies in the Argyll and Bute District Archives in Lochgilphead. Two leather-bound tomes written by John Colville, a maltster in Campbeltown, cover the periods from 1814 to 1819 and 1823 to 1826. In the first volume 127 names appear on a regular basis; of these 68 are women. Given that Campbeltown was a thriving port at the time, the inference must be that women undertook whisky-making as one of their regular domestic chores; just another job that had to be carried out alongside many others.

The scale of their operations can be ascertained form the frequency of their dealings with Colville. Most of the women appeared to have had a barter arrangement with Colville whereby the value of the malt they took from him was returned in liquid form. In this way Colville received a commodity of a higher value than the price of his barley and the women were able to sell on their excess production for ready cash. In 1820, Jenny Currie delivered whisky to Colville on 23 occasions in quantities ranging from two pints to 13 pints (a boll of malt was then priced at £2 16 shillings).

In the second volume 76 customers are listed, 19 of them being carried over from the first book. Of this total, 46 were male and 30 female, but they were all illicit distillers. Flory MacTaggart uplifted malt on 34 occasions, with amounts ranging from nine pecks to double the quantity at one boll and two pecks (see appendix 6 on page 144). Seventy-one of these illicit distillers are named with their localities so that the geographical spread of the trade throughout Kintyre is revealed (see appendix 4 on page 138). Furthermore, Robert Armour, the Campbeltown plumber who also made stills on the side, serviced the illicit distillers when legal distilling was non-existent in the area between 1797 and 1817. This was due to legislative changes in the law that increased the duty to £9 per gallon of still volume. Legal distillers simply went underground and refused to cough up. Within three years 292 stills had been confiscated and destroyed in Campbeltown alone. Illicit distilling in Kintyre mushroomed and women were as active in the trade as their male counterparts. Armour's records cover the period from May 1811 to September 1817. They show that he supplied stills and other equipment to over 58 women, sometimes in partnership with others, and in 42 instances to mixed groups. One hundred sales were made to males alone. Armour's handicraft was in widespread use throughout much of Argyll, Gigha and south-west Arran. These illicit stills were worked hard and Armour was a man much in demand.

Eventually, in 1814, the government banned stills of less than 500 gallons of volume in the Highlands, but the move backfired and no large-scale ventures were established in Kintyre. A year later the tax on still volume was abolished but the new duty of 9 shillings four and a halfpenny on every gallon of new spirit replaced it and nothing changed. Further legal tinkering amounted to nothing until 1823 when the Excise Act was passed. For an annual licence fee of £10, plus reduced rates of duty on spirits and exports, an illicit distiller could finally go legal with a commercially viable operation.

The sheer concentration of illicit distilling activity in and around Campbeltown during this period was immediately utilised. Only one legal distillery had been re-established in the town before 1823, namely Campbeltown in the Longrow, (the street that runs down through the heart of the town from the north to its centre by the harbour) but many more were to follow. The town became the distilling capital of Argyll, and some would argue Scotland, as the number of operations established during the 19th century exceeded anything Dufftown could boast during the same period. By the time the Ordnance Survey first visited the area in 1868, their map of the town clearly shows 19 in existence and of a scale that was worthy of mention. What is not apparent from this picture is that since 1823 there had been numerous other concerns that had either failed or were of a size that did not merit mention. When Barnard visited the town in 1886 he deemed it necessary to visit 21 distilleries, although there were others operating at that time.

There is no clearer example anywhere in Scotland of how the 1823 legislation regarding distilling went on to create enormous wealth and prosperity from totally illicit origins. Furthermore, the role that the womenfolk of Argyll played in this was fundamental to the town's success and to the creation of several distilling dynasties that were to dominate the trade in Campbeltown for over 100 years. The eventual failure of the majority of these distillers is another story that I will not relate here. But as a footnote to this chapter, it is curious how the only truly small-scale family-owned and operated malt whisky distillery still in existence in its original urban location is Springbank in Campbeltown. And the head of the family that owns it is directly descended from the Mitchell family who went legal in 1828. Their names: Hugh, Archibald, John, William … and Mary.

CHAPTER THREE

ISLAY

The Kildalton Distilleries

THE KILDALTON DISTILLERIES all lie along a three-mile (five-km) stretch of the A846 to the east of Port Ellen, the town established by Walter Frederick Campbell in 1821 and named after his first wife, Eleanor. Port Ellen sits at the base of the neck of the land separating the peninsula of Oa from the old parish of Kildalton that sits along the island's south coast beyond the reach of the public road. A Caledonian MacBrayne ferry from Kennacraig arrives each day throughout the year at Port Ellen, the main harbour in the area. To ignore the remote and beautiful landscape of the Oa would be to miss a fascinating chapter in the history of whisky. The Oa's deep inland glens and hidden caves became the source of a great deal of work for the Excise in the first half of the 19th century.

Operating from Port Ellen the Excise officers had the miserable job of searching out the smugglers' bothies in all weathers. They were not the hardiest of people – almost all of them came from the mainland and they were regular petitioners to the Board of Excise for two weeks 'sick' leave. That the Excise almost always came across illicit distillation in the same places says as much for their enthusiasm as it does for the suitability of the terrain for the distillers. The extent of illicit distilling in Islay at this time can be seen from the list of persons against whom the Excise took

action at the turn of the century. (See appendix 3 on page 134).

The road to the Oa runs past the Port Ellen bonded warehouses, eventually running out at Killeyan, or Killain. At least one of the caves along the coast near Killeyan was often used for storing malt, while a little further north at Giol more extensive operations were possible – with eight bushels of green malt and 250 gallons (1,135 litres) of wash confiscated in one instance. On the very point of the land, at the Mull of Oa, stands the gaunt memorial to the American sailors who lost their lives in 1918 when the *Tuscania* sank off the coast. There were so many bodies washed ashore that the floor maltings in Port Ellen were used as the mortuary.

Other haunts were Cragabus and Stremnishmore. With the help of the Customs Cutter SS *Chichester*, the Excise finally caught some distillers redhanded in February 1850 in a cave near Lower Killeyan. Although they made off, they were all known faces whom the Excise later arrested. The Excise reported that they:

… were obliged to descend over a precipice about 70 feet deep and during the time they were descending the smugglers fled by some outlet among the rocks which was not easy to discover; their names are Alexander

McCuaig of Upper Killain, Donald McGibon of Lower Killain and Neil McGibon his brother. There were also in the cave five large casks containing about 300 gallons of wash ready for distillation which they completely destroyed.

After their arrest the men made a plea, albeit unlikely, to the effect that they 'had no concern whatever with the private distillery but merely went into the cave by way of curiosity and they happened to be there when the officers came but they are willing to come forward and prove against the real party concerned ... Duncan Campbell of Giol, John McIntyre and Neil McIntyre his brother both residing in Glenegadale Moor ... ' It didn't work and the men, unable to pay a steep £30 fine each, were jailed at Inveraray for three months despite the magnanimity of the Excise in asking for clemency due to their extreme poverty.

The secret to the existence of Islay's distilleries is the sea. In the late 1820s the laird, Walter Frederick Campbell, recognised that only with strong sea links to the mainland would the agricultural reforms that his forebears had created stand any chance of survival. He started a regular steamer service between Glasgow, Tarbert on Loch Fyne, West Loch Tarbert, Islay and

Skye with a couple of passenger steamers called *Maid of Islay* (I and II). This service was to be developed over the remainder of the century and was the most vital social and commercial link the island had with the outside world.

Safe anchorages and better access by road and sea eventually led to the successful distillers consolidating themselves on the other side of Port Ellen. For years supply boats have made their way into the relatively sheltered anchorages at Ardbeg, Lagavulin, Laphroaig and Port Ellen itself. In July 2002, Sir Chay Blyth, sailing in the annual Classic Malts Cruise, formally opened the Port Ellen pontoons for private sailing yachts – a much needed boost to the local tourist economy. The impact of recreational sailing in these waters cannot be overestimated. Every July the Classic Malts Cruise, sponsored by Diageo, sails from Oban to Islay, then up to Skye and back to Oban before returning to Lagavulin (see appendix 5 on page 140). During that time a considerable amount of money is injected by the flotilla and Diageo into the island communities.

The approach from the sea to Lagavulin bay is dominated by the impressive outline of Dunyveg Castle and presents a challenge to any sailor. It must have been an even more formidable prospect for the enemies of the Macdonalds and even now the ruins dwarf any passing boats.

The coast road runs past all the Kildalton distilleries and at its easterly limit lies Tallant. One is tempted to think that this is where the ubiquitous Johnstons distilled for the best part of a century, but they were at the other Tallant on the far side of the Laggan Bog. It seems that the last John Johnston to operate there never did so on a profitable commercial scale and he was described by the Excise in 1838 as being in 'very low circumstances'. Frequently reported to the Board of Excise for undue reductions in stock, he seems to have been generous with his drams for visiting workmen (' … generally great dram drinkers … ') and small farmers bringing grain 'for sale' around New Year when as much as two gallons of malt were once consumed!

This may have been one of the reasons why Johnston was soon in ' … embarrassed circumstances … ', but with an output of only 220 gallons (1,000 litres) a week, he was never a match for the bigger and better situated distilleries along the Kildalton coast. Although his business folded around 1852, his brother Donald and his son Alexander were to be successful distillers figuring prominently in Laphroaig's development. At Tallant in Kildalton, however, there was an exceptional smithy thanks to the local bog water it used for tempering.

Between Tallant and the shore the famous Kildalton Cross stands within the cemetery where John Campbell, one of the descendants of Duncan Campbell of Ardmore was returned for burial from Mull in the 1860s where he had been Chamberlain to the Duke of Argyll.

Alexander 'Sandy' Johnston took Laphroaig into the 20th century before control passed into the hands of his sisters and nephew.

The circumstances surrounding the funeral are worth retelling, because they display how different versions of a perfectly straightforward local event can arise from nothing more than a desire to tell a good yarn. Campbell's body was brought down from Mull by

Key to defunct Kildalton distilleries

1 Port Ellen
2 Ardenistiel
3 Ardmore
4 Malt Mill

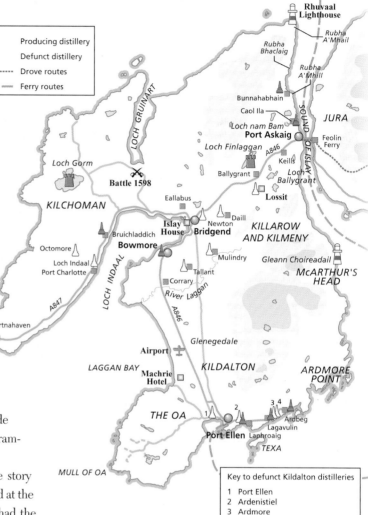

Key to map labels:

- Producing distillery
- Defunct distillery
- Drove routes
- Ferry routes

Rhuvaal Lighthouse
Rubha A'Mhail
Rubha Bhaclaig
Rubha A'Mhill
Bunnahabhain
Caol Ila
JURA
Loch nam Bam
Port Askaig
Feolin Ferry
Loch Finlaggan
A846
Keills
Loch Gorm
Ballygrant
Loch Ballygrant
Battle 1598
Eallabus
Lossit
KILCHOMAN
Islay House
Bridgend
Newton
Daill
KILLAROW AND KILMENY
Bruichladdich
Bowmore
Octomore
Mulindry
Gleann Choireadail
Loch Indaal
Port Charlotte
Tallant
McARTHUR'S HEAD
Corrary
River Laggan
A847
LOCH INDAAL
Portnahaven
Glenegedale
A846
Airport
KILDALTON
ARDMORE POINT
LAGGAN BAY
Machrie Hotel
THE OA
3 4
2
Ardbeg
1
Lagavulin
Port Ellen
Laphroaig
TEXA
MULL OF OA

Key to defunct Kildalton distilleries
1 Port Ellen
2 Ardenistiel
3 Ardmore
4 Malt Mill

steamer to the tiny bay of Clas Uig beyond Ardmore Point, where the coffin was unloaded and carried up the rough hillside by the local gentlemen, mostly Campbells and MacNeills. Provisions were also brought from Mull for all the mourners, so that a banquet could be held before the boat returned.

But after the passage of many years, a local version of the funeral slowly emerged which incorrectly claimed that Campbell's body had arrived in Port Ellen, to be borne down the coast road by a relay of villagers along the route. The length of the journey, and the burden of the coffin necessitated 'wee rests' along the way which were made doubly pleasurable by some justifiable dram-drinking.

The unfortunate outcome of this, so the story goes, is that when the villagers finally arrived at the cemetery, they found that they no longer had the

Port Ellen Distillery staff, 1906.

coffin. It is claimed that on retracing their steps they came upon the coffin lying by the roadside just up the brae from Surnaig House at Lagavulin. This is undoubtedly a fabrication, but its retelling is none the worse for it.

A more factual, but equally interesting tale involving the Campbells arose when the old family home at Ardmore was converted into a barn after the building of the new house in 1873. Being descended from one such as Duncan Campbell, the entire family was extremely musical and they were all renowned fiddlers. On raising the wooden floor to replace it with newly-invented concrete, a remarkable sight was beheld – the entire floor space was filled with clean cattle skulls. Any macabre conclusions that arose were dashed when

it was explained that Duncan Campbell had placed them there in the belief that the skulls made the floor a better sounding board!

The present-day existence of the Kildalton distilleries can largely be attributed to the lairds who possessed the parish lands in the 18th, 19th and early 20th centuries. The Campbells brought agrarian reform to the island and when the Islay estate was sold in the middle of the 19th century, the new owner of Kildalton, James Morrison, sold that part of his estate to John Ramsay who maintained and developed the distilling activity at Port Ellen and along the coast. Ramsay's shrewd business mind and his pioneering export trade to the United States did much to secure the future of distilling in the parish.

Clas Uig bay, Islay, 1984. The landing point for Chamberlain John Campbell's burial party from Mull can be seen clearly beyond the Alystra's anchorage.

Ardbeg

NOT UNTIL 1977, when the Canadian company Hiram Walker & Sons finally gained control of Ardbeg, was the long family connection with the MacDougalls finally severed. Since 1798 the family had resided as farmers and distillers in the area, being tenants in Ardbeg, Airigh nam Beist and half of Lagavulin farms. Distilling operations had been going on in the area prior to the sequestration of Alexander Stewart in 1794, but were not restarted on a commercial basis until 1815 by Duncan MacDougall's son John. In 1886, when Alfred Barnard was collecting information for his book *The Whisky Distilleries of the United Kingdom* for *Harper's Gazette* of London, he reported that by 1835 output was around 500 gallons (2,270 litres) a year.

The financial backing for the distillery appears to have come from the Glasgow merchant Thomas Buchanan Jnr, for in 1838 Walter Frederick Campbell granted a lease for the Ardbeg farm with two acres to Buchanan for 57 years and disposed of the distillery for £1,800. John's son Alexander had by then taken over the distilling operations, and leased the farm at Airigh nam Beist for a yearly rental of £45, trading as Alexander MacDougall & Company. Alexander appears to have been a character as Barnard recalls:

… His clannishness was intense. This Highland virtue he prominently exhibited on a certain occasion, when he discovered in court that some unknown namesake was pronounced by the judge 'Guilty' and sentence of a fine or imprisonment was imposed, Mr McDougall interposed the statement 'that it was impossible that a McDougall could do anything wrong' and therefore he would pay the fine!

Some of his employees were not so generous towards him, for he spent the latter part of his adult life confined to a wheelchair and, according to the Excise was therefore 'more easily imposed upon by his servants'. The disability led to his sister Margaret joining her brother as a licensee, and handing over management of the distillery to Colin Hay, the son of Walter Frederick Campbell's coachman, some three years before Alexander died in 1853. Margaret and her sister Flora then acquired lets 'of the farms of Ardbeg and half Lagavulin' in 1851 from James Brown, trustee

Ardbeg Distillery, 1984.

for the sequestrated estate of Walter Frederick Campbell. The lease clearly states that the sisters were 'Co-partners carrying business at Ardbeg as Distillers under the firm of Alexander McDougall & Company ... ' The true extent of their involvement in the distillery proper can only be surmised, suffice to say that Margaret was 63 when she was granted the lease!

Under Hay, Ardbeg grew into a small community based around the distillery and he estimated that in 1853 there were some 200 people living in and around Ardbeg and Lagavulin as similar villages had sprung up at the neighbouring distilleries comprising shops and other services to meet the day-to-day needs of the community. He became sole proprietor after the deaths of the MacDougall sisters but trained one of his two sons, Colin Elliot, as a distiller while backing still came from the Buchanans. His other son Walter became a doctor and remained a partner in the distillery. At the time of Barnard's visit in 1886 the inventory included a 16-feet diameter cast iron mashtun some five feet in depth, eight washbacks of 8,000 gallons (36,320 litres) each, one wash still of 4,000 gallons (18,160 litres) and one spirit still of 3,000 gallons (1,362 litres) producing a then prodigious 250,000 gallons (1.135 million litres) per year with a workforce of 60 people.

By 1888, a new lease was granted to Alexander Wilson Gray Buchanan (heir to Thomas Buchanan Jnr), and Colin Elliot Hay which included rights to the Ardbeg pier costing £100 per year. Four years into the lease Colin Hay was forced to write to Peter Reid, the Ramsay's factor at Port Ellen, claiming that this was 'a very heavy charge in these times of diminished trade ... It amounts to 7d per ton on all the goods brought in and sent out by us,' implying that some 3,200 tons of barley, casks, whisky and sundries were passing up and down the pier each year. This is an interesting statement given that John Ramsay, with only a few

Walter Frederick Campbell, the last Campbell laird of Islay.

years to live, had become increasingly frustrated with the poor performance of the steamer service which was by then being run by David Hutcheson's nephew, David MacBrayne.

In August 1890 Ramsay pleaded with Charles Morrison to support the establishment of a new company and before the year was out a prospectus for the Islay Steam Packet Company had been distributed to a number of provisional directors including distillers and landowners on Islay. Colin Hay of Ardbeg was listed as one of those directors who was, according to the prospectus, prepared to 'supply a better steamboat service than has for some years been provided for the islands of Islay and Jura'. The prospectus, of course, failed to reveal that Colin Hay was then at an advanced age and had ceased active farming at Ardilestry in 1889. However, Ramsay's gamble paid off and MacBrayne bowed to his demands to increase the level of service to the islands. The new company had no need to come into existence but the effort Ramsay expended in the affair must have been considerable. In January 1892 he died, leaving his estate, under the management of his factor, Peter Reid, to his son Captain Iain Ramsay.

In the last decade of the 19th century the distillery was managed by Colin Elliot Hay who had a distiller, John MacMillan, from a large and well-known local family, under him. One of Hay's cousins, Alexander Hay MacDougall acted as clerk and lived with his two sisters in a house up the brae from the distillery. Colin Elliot's domestic arrangements were similarly dominated by women: his wife allowed her unmarried sister, a Miss McGilvray, to live with them.

The community nature of Ardbeg at that time is obvious from the terms of the new lease which was granted in 1900 to Hay's sons for ' … All and whole the Distillery of Ardbeg … also the farm of Ardbeg … excepting from the said farm the School and Teacher's house of Ardbeg … '

The village at that time housed the families of over 40 distillery workers along with two resident Excise officers but only the Hays, the MacDougalls and the Excisemen benefited from piped water and flush toilets. The rest of the village had three dry closets and even the village school (with around 100 pupils) had to make do with another two of the same.

Colin Hay died on 10th of February 1899 around the same time as John MacMillan. His position was taken by a former trainee clerk, a Mr Campbell, who was to manage Ardbeg until the Great War when he left to serve in the 8th Battalion of the Argyll and Sutherland Highlanders. He returned after the war to find that his job had been 'permanently filled' and after that a succession of managers came and went until the 1930s.

In 1902 the Ardbeg distillery business was incorporated as a limited company and survived the vicissitudes of the Great War, the General Strike, prohibition and the Depression despite its remote

Captain Iain Ramsay finally took over the Kildalton Estate at the age of 27 after the death of his father in 1892 and his mother Lucy in 1905. He was forced to sell all his distilleries – Ardbeg, Lagavulin, Laphroaig and Port Ellen – in order to maintain his dwindling estate.

The Ardbeg filling store c 1812 with Willie McKerrell (rear) and Hugh McLean (foreground).

location. By 1919, the company had incorporated their agent's business, Buchanan, Wilson & Co Ltd, with a combined share capital of £20,000 and plans were in place to increase the capital to £50,000 by, as recorded by Colin Elliot, 'getting friends in "The Trade" into the business'.

Under Hay, business was conducted in a meticulous fashion. This is transparent from the correspondence ledgers which still survive, on site, to this day. By sifting through them it is possible to understand how he must have spent much of his time. As a single malt, Ardbeg was available to any private customer who had a credit account with the distillery. One such customer was Alice M Disney of Kingston Hill, Surrey. On the 20th May 1920, Hay wrote to her:

Dear Madam,

We have your letter of the 17th inst. We can supply you with a small Octave, old 'Ardbeg', direct from the Distillery, as before. The price (Duty-Paid), is now £4. 0s. 3d, per proof gallon. 'F.O.B' here, and we could get it cleared for you, at about 16 Under Proof strength. If Bottles would be more convenient for your Cellar, we can order on, through our Glasgow Office, bottled 'Ardbeg'; the strength of this, has to be 30 Under Proof, present price, (Duty-Paid), = £137. 0. 6d. a case of 12 bottles, (2 Gallons), 'F.O.B' Glasgow.

On hearing from you, we shall be pleased, to send on the 'Ardbeg', either in cask, direct from here, or in bottles, from Glasgow, as you may wish. The bottled 'Ardbeg', is same quality, and age, as you would get it, from Distillery, but weaker in strength.

We are,
Yours faithfully,
Colin E Hay

To which the clearly otherwise-occupied Mrs Disney responded on a hastily scribbled note:

Rossie
Gloucester Road
Kingston Mill
Surrey
June 14th, 1920
Dear Sir,

In answer to your letter of May 20th respecting whisky, I should like to have a small octave old Ardbeg at £4/3 per Proof Gallon sent me 16 under proof strength as soon as possible.

Yours faithfully,
(Mrs) Alice M Disney

Against this backdrop of 'business as usual' the British economy was struggling. The miners' strike of 1920 was bad for business as Hay sourced coal supplies from any available merchant. On the 11th of June, he received a quote from Alexander S Millar & Co, of 19 St Vincent Place:

Miners giving trouble. 43sh per ton Fifeshire Splint Coal with shipping at 18/6d per ton Ardbeg.

But Hay and the Buchanan family pursued the purchase of the distillery lands and associated fields throughout 1920 and 1921 via Iain Ramsay's chartered accountants, Robert Macfarlan of 149 West George Street, Glasgow. After a good deal of coming and going on the negotiated price, Arbeg was eventually sold by Ramsay in 1922. It was the third of the Kildalton distilleries which he was forced to let go in order to maintain his depressed estate. Ardbeg and its lands changed hands for £19,000 with £9,000 being paid as cash with interest at 5% per annum from Whitsun 1922, and £10,000 being secured in the form of a Bond and Disposition to be reduced to £5,000 by 1927, and finally written off by 1932. Such were the economics of the depression.

The management of the distillery soon fell to a Mr Calder who more or less replaced Colin Elliot Hay as the company presence at Ardbeg. For many years Hay had been fighting alcoholism and other health problems which some observers claimed were exacerbated by his wife's treatment of him, which was often publicly demeaning. Hay died on the 19th of March, 1928, aged 61 and was buried at Stracathro in the east of Scotland. Curiously, on that very same day the 238-acre farm of Ardbeg was let to Archibald McAllister of Ardtalla for 11 years at a rental of £170 per annum; the outgoing tenant being John McNicol who had been in the farm since Whitsunday, 1915.

However, the link between farm and distillery was clearly something that the company no longer saw as desirable. In a letter of the 3rd August 1928 Alexander Hay MacDougall clearly states that:

' ... we only had three inquiries and one offer for Ardbeg Farm and I certainly think it is pretty evident we were fortunate in getting any offer at all for the place, looking to the very large number of Farms and Holdings on the market for sometime back. Of course, the only alternative to getting a let for the Farm would be that we would have to take over the whole burdens, financial, and otherwise, ourselves, a thing which, if possible, we would wish to avoid.'

And no wonder. The distilling industry was no longer

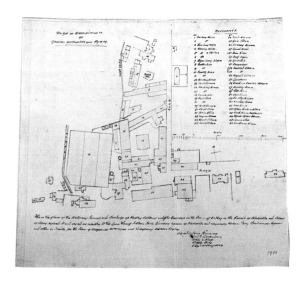

A survey plan of Ardbeg from 1900.

Carts were frequently brought in from surrounding farms to do distillery work.

one which was tied to the croft and in explaining the circumstances surrounding the letting of the farm, MacDougall revealed a great deal more about the matter:

'It has come to our knowledge that the late Tenant, McNicol, endeavoured to prejudice McAllister, against taking the place, and also did his best to spoil the sale of some of McAllister's Cattle, at Stirling, by spreading a Report among buyers that his Dairy Stock were infected with Abortion, a particularly mean thing to do, after practically robbing the man, here.'

MacDougall may have rued his sentiments when it transpired later that year that McAllister was in a desperate financial state with the bank pressing for bankruptcy. The matter was eventually resolved by relieving him of the farm tenancy towards the end of 1929 when everyone involved in the fiasco had lost patience with him.

Curiously it was not too long before MacDougall, who was briefly manager of Ardbeg in the early 1930s, left the employment of the company under something of a cloud when accusations were made against him and a female clerkess regarding the company's books.

But the running of the distillery involved not only farming and tenancy matters, but also the logistical management of incoming and outgoing shipping and pier maintenance. The Ardbeg pier was a familiar sight to the many puffers which plied the West Coast and Clyde waters from their base on Glasgow's Broomielaw. These vessels were the container transports of their day

and were absolutely vital in maintaining the commercial highway that linked the remote island distilleries with their mainland markets.

Vessels such as the paddle steamers *Lochiel* and *Clydesdale*, and puffers like *Tuscan*, *Gael*, and *Glenshira* were all frequent visitors to Ardbeg. Sometimes the weather was so foul that cargo bound for Laphroaig (which was not serviced with a pier) had to be offloaded at Ardbeg and carted down the parish road to Laphroaig. This was a 'service' that Calder was content to render, so long as Laphroaig were prepared to arrange for the carting, which was something that Ian Hunter (the owner of Laphroaig between 1924 and 1954) was a little lax in arranging.

Sometimes the puffers never made it. On the 4th December, 1925, *The Serb*, built by J&J Hay Ltd of Kirkintilloch in 1916, and one of the most familiar of the West-coast puffers, was shipwrecked on the rocks at the entry to Ardbeg carrying a full cargo of barley and malt. A letter from the grain merchants to the distillery reveals the extent of the incident:

The puffer Serb offloads at Loch Gruinart, Islay.

'We regret very much to learn of the disaster which befell this steamer last week. We had hoped that there would be a chance of getting some of the cargo out of her, but we have learned that she has slipped off the rocks and is now completely submerged. It is gratifying to know, however, that the crew have been all saved.'

The risks which these crews ran were very much greater than is the case today when hardly any barley arrives by sea. The Port Ellen Maltings, owned by Diageo, now supplies the island's distilleries with their entire malt requirement. In Colin Elliot Hay's day the shipments were often of malt and barley that had been grown as far afield as Karachi, Australia and Canada and Hay was particularly fond of Australian Chevalier which he claimed was amongst 'the finest I have ever seen'.

Alexander Campbell, the son of the manager who found he had lost his job on returning from the Great War, was born at the manager's house in 1901 and before his death was able to recall the arrival of the these vessels:

'There was seldom a day but there was a vessel of some kind at the "big" pier which could berth any of them. I can remember one large two-masted steamer going slightly off the normal channel into Ardbeg bay and landing on a rock right out in front of our house. This necessitated unloading the cargo into small boats and bringing it into the "wee" pier just below our house.
Also MacBrayne's cargo boat called at Ardbeg twice weekly (Tuesdays and Fridays) with mixed cargo which included empty casks and yeast in bags or casks, and of course took on full casks of whisky and bags of dried draff for making animal feed such as oil cake.
'When a boat came in with coal or barley all available farm carts around the area were employed to supplement the regular distillery cartage.'

According to Alexander Campbell, by the end of the 1920s the decline in Ardbeg as a community was 'noticeable'. Having returned to the island in 1928 as medical officer for Kildalton and Oa, many of the people he had grown up with became his patients and he was familiar with almost everybody at the distillery. With the passing of Colin Elliot Hay, the company presence diminished at the distillery and his house was let out to paying guests before being converted to workers' accommodation.

As the years passed the distillery languished with its fortunes tied to the wellbeing of the whisky trade in general. Alexander MacDougall & Co continued to own and manage Ardbeg until its liquidation in 1959 when Ardbeg Distillery Ltd was formed, being superseded in 1973 by the Ardbeg Distillery Trust comprising the Distillers Company Limited (DCL) and Hiram Walker & Sons Ltd.

That so many of the industry's big players had taken an interest in this remote island distillery was testament to the way in which Islay malt was regarded (and still is) as an essential ingredient in the blender's portfolio. Blended Scotch whisky is constructed from numerous component malts and a healthy proportion of neutral grain whisky. As a single malt Ardbeg had always had a small but fanatical band of followers (like Mrs Disney of Surrey!) although the old-fashioned business of sending octaves by rail to private customers in the south of England waned and eventually ceased altogether. The Second World War created restrictions on the manufacture of malt whisky and as the declining national network of rail transport was nationalised, giving way to motor transport, so sea-borne supply gradually diminished. With the advent of the roll-on/roll-off ferry service to Islay in 1968, the puffers and cargo coasters were doomed and Ardbeg (along with the rest of the Islay distilleries) had to transport its fillings by road haulier for the first time in its existence.

Ardbeg Distillery kilns, 1984.

A traditional distillery in such a location as Ardbeg, with an output, almost all of which went for blending, would obviously have struggled to survive the economic strictures of the 1970s and when the Hiram Walker-owned Allied Distillers took over the plant at a cost of £300,000 in 1976, only six years of production were enjoyed before the distillery was mothballed with the loss of 18 jobs. This more or less finished Ardbeg as a distillery village.

In April 1984 Don Raitt, the then manager could only parry the question of re-opening with the heartfelt comment, 'Well, we are spending money on the place.' The maintenance helped to give a semblance of normality, but there was a ghostly feel to the place and the lack of industry gave little hope for the future. The malting floors lay abandoned and one of the large Victorian bonds to the east of the distillery, which is clearly visible in a surveyor's plan of 1900 (see page 36), was razed to the ground. The pagodas underwent external re-cladding but the stench of mashing and the aromatic ethers of the stillhouse were missing. Would they ever return?

Five years after I made my 1984 trip the situation had changed little but in 1989 a corporate makeover led to the distillery coming under the same owners, Allied

Distillers, as close neighbour Laphroaig. That meant that the company had two distilleries in their malt portfolio producing similar types of malt whisky. Despite the fact that Laphroaig was the brand that Allied wanted to maintain and develop on a worldwide basis, manager Iain Henderson was asked not only to act as caretaker of Ardbeg for the foreseeable future, but also to commence small-scale distilling again.

The production was essentially for fillings for the blenders but some of it was laid down. It seems strange that when Allied decided to close the distillery in 1982, the man who made the decision was also one of Ardbeg's biggest fans. When Jim Murray interviewed Alistair Cunningham after he had retired from the company he was wildly enthusiastic about the whisky:

'I spoke to the marketing people for years and years, and they thought me a few shillings short of a pound because I said: "Here's Ardbeg, here's something unique." It would have been something I would like to have seen.

'It's heaven's own nectar, you know. Different to anything else. If you knew exactly the amount to take each day, you could live forever.'

Allied's problem was a corporate one in that they had a large portfolio of distilleries to consider in their planning and Ardbeg simply did not feature in it. The future was undoubtedly bleak and in 1992 Jim Murray was moved to remark, when writing in the *Scotsman* about the distillery's future: 'Tragically for Ardbeg and us all, that means perhaps until next century custodianship behind the warehouses' triple locks.'

By the mid-1990s Allied Distillers were making no secret of the fact that Ardbeg was up for sale at the right price to a suitable bidder and a number of parties registered their interest in the distillery. Among them was Glenmorangie plc, owner of the Scotland's favourite malt whisky, Glenmorangie, and the much-admired Glen Moray from Speyside. The company was not an industry giant in the way that Allied was, but that was precisely why the deal made such sense.

Glenmorangie's scale was an ideal fit for Ardbeg. Here was a company with a small, popular malt whisky portfolio which did not possess a large corporate mentality; a 'can-do' company which saw the distillery not for what it had become, but rather for what it could be.

Run down: yes. In need of huge investment and capital outlay: certainly. But also they recognised that as a malt it had a fantastic reputation, and had been grossly under-produced, under-sold and neglected for far too long.

Glenmorangie's acquisition of Ardbeg in 1997 was heralded in the trade press and throughout the whisky industry as an extremely significant development. There were other interested parties but none of them could match the Glenmorangie package. With Glenmorangie from the Northern Highlands, and Glen Moray from Speyside already in the fold, Ardbeg's inclusion created a distinct regional diversity which would allow the product to be properly marketed and exploited. But the acquisition meant that a great deal

of planning had to be put in place to bring Ardbeg up to industry standards, not only in terms of production practices and technology, but also for health and safety requirements. The shopping list was daunting, but between March and May 1997, Glenmorangie had a major number of changes made. These included new heating tanks, steam lines, feed tanks, a malt conveyor and dust aspirator and a new roof on warehouse number three. A further three washbacks were replaced in Oregon pine. The total cost was £250,000 with another £50,000 spent on new electrical cabling and wiring.

Conscious of the impact that visitors can make to distillery employment and turnover, one of the kilns was converted at a cost £725,000 in time for the 1998 season to incorporate a café, shop and visitor centre. In short, almost everything had to be revisited and reviewed in order to bring the distillery into the new millennium. Ed Dodson, later manager of Glen Moray Distillery, spent six months after the acquisition setting up the processes prior to the arrival of Stuart Thomson who had been appointed manager.

Stuart had been assistant manager at Glen Moray since 1993 and prior to that had worked for 12 years at Glenmorangie where his father had been assistant manager. Although he once wanted to be a stockbroker, Stuart has spent all his working life in the whisky trade and did not regret the move. 'The location is fantastic and it's a wonderful place for children to grow up in.' His wife Jackie was given the remit to commission and manage the visitor centre and accompanying facilities. With a varied and consistently excellent menu it is now an ideal place for Islay whisky enthusiasts, after visiting Laphroaig and Lagavulin, to stop for a meal.

Also during 1999 a new mashtun was installed and raised off the floor by three metres to facilitate draff transfer and drainage. Ingeniously, it is still skinned in

*Stuart Thomson (upper left);
stencilling a cask end (right);
the Old Kiln Café (lower left)*

the original cast iron sections from which the old mashtun was constructed. New lauter stirring gear and a control panel completed the renewals to the tune of £300,000 – which formed part of the overall expenditure of £1.4 million spent on new plant and machinery since the acquisition.

During 2000, a new condenser and intermediate spirit receiver were installed and the faithful 50-year-old spirit still replaced with a replica. (The original now stands at the entrance to the car park at the gable end

of one of the old malting floors.) But perhaps more meaningfully, many of the former Ardbeg workers who thought they would never see the distillery producing again, were back.

Alex Woodrow was born in 1945 at Duich and at the age of two moved to Ardbeg where his father worked in the malt barns. Educated in the village school that Eliza Ramsay had helped to establish almost a century before, Alex grew up in the distillery village and still remembers the shop where, 'you could buy just about

Alex Woodrow, stillman, Ardbeg

worked under six managers in all and is currently one of the stillmen.

Malcolm Rennie was born in Stirling in 1961 and moved to Islay in 1974 when his father started work as a cooper at Bunnahabhain Distillery. Educated at Bowmore, he went to work at Bunnahabhain in 1979 before joining the Merchant Navy for two and a half years during which time he 'went everywhere'. After returning to Islay in 1982 he started work as a mashman at Bruichladdich before being made redundant in 1995. Glenmorangie plc's purchase of Ardbeg has meant a great deal to the likes of Malcolm, who is married with a daughter and a baby son. 'It was looking pretty bleak at one time, but it's turned out all right in the end,' he told me before confiding that his favourite dram was the 1975.

Alec Livingstone is one of the other mashmen at Ardbeg who has also been employed at another Islay distillery as well as spending some time at sea. Born in 1954 he worked in the malt lofts at Laphroaig before joining the Royal Navy between 1976 and 1985. For a time he also worked on the fishing boats in Devon before returning home for a spell of one year at Ardbeg under Don Raitt. He remembers the way it used to be but commented that, 'The characters have gone from this trade. They simply aren't there any more.' That may be true of the industry in general, but he cannot be referring to his own workmates, in particular, "The Gow", Hamish Gillespie, stillman. He has worked on Islay all his life coming into the distillery in 1989 after working on the Islay Estate's farm and at Woodrows,

anything at all'. At that time the village consisted of over 20 households and after Alex left secondary school in Port Ellen in 1960 he started work on Ardbeg Farm where he remained for the next four years. After that he began work at the distillery and has remained there ever since, experiencing the highs and the lows, the periods of production and the long lay-offs. He is the longest-serving employee at the distillery, having the builders. And it is heartening to see the likes of 32-year-old Douglas Bowman from Port Ellen, who has been working at Ardbeg as a warehouse operator for the last four years after leaving the Royal Navy.

The sea became an escape route for many of Islay's unemployed distillery workers who were able to make a living by joining up. That many of today's workforce have come 'Westering home' to Islay seems a fitting testament to Ardbeg's heritage where the lives of the MacDougalls, the Hays, the Ramsays and hundreds of distillery workers' families were once so irrevocably tied to the rhythms of the sea.

Ardbeg Distillery

By Port Ellen, Islay, Argyll PA42 7DU
Tel: 01496 302244 Fax: 01496 302040
www.ardbeg.com
Owners: Glenmorangie plc
Manager: Stuart Thomson

WHEN I first visited Ardbeg back in 1984 it was in a forlorn state. The then manager, Don Raitt was overseeing basic care and maintenance on behalf of the owners, Hiram Walker, who had all but washed their hands of the place. To come upon it today fairly takes the breath away. The buildings are re-roofed and whitewashed and the distinctive Ardbeg green is used to good effect.

Glenmorangie's extensive renovations and re-equipment of the distillery is evident almost everywhere. In the Old Kiln Café, food is served to a very high standard and the retail items available are of a similar quality. The interior still reeks of peat and the adjoining exhibition spaces are well utilised.

A short walk down to the shore brings you to the small pier that Colin Hay found such a financial burden in 1892, sticking prominently into the mouth of Loch an't Sailein. Nowadays it is likely to see a flotilla of small craft from Northern Ireland tie up for the day as daytrippers descend on Ardbeg for a pre-planned visit.

What immediately strikes the frequent visitor to this part of Islay is how much the distillery has revitalised the area. Canny visitors flock here at lunchtime to enjoy the fruits of the Old Kiln Café kitchen and the part which Ardbeg plays in the Islay Festival of Music and Malt and other social events is significant. In many ways, Ardbeg is the best possible place to return to on this island whisky trail as it shows exactly what can be done with an unwanted distillery when a company with vision has the opportunity to develop it.

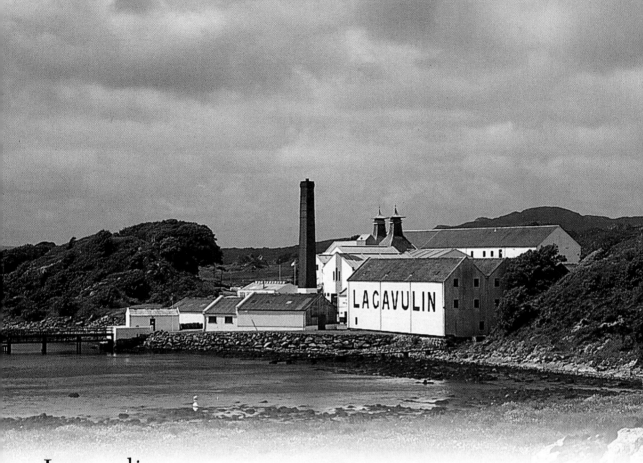

Lagavulin

LAGAVULIN can lay claim to being one of the oldest distilleries in Scotland – it is almost certainly built on the oldest site of established distilling activity on Islay. When he passed through Barnard was informed that at around 1742 there were 'ten small and separate smuggling bothies for the manufacture of "moonlight", which when working presented anything but a true picture of "still life", and were all subsequently absorbed into one establishment, the whole work not making more than a few thousand gallons per annum.' Firm evidence of this appears in an inventory taken in June 1784 of the belongings of Duncan Campbell of Ardmore who had been the tacksman for the Miln farm and half of Lagavulin.

Campbell, whose family had been Chamberlains to Campbell of Cawdor in Kildalton, is reputed to have got into difficulties following the ban on distilling on Islay in 1783 and the introduction of the Wash Act the next year. He fled the island and being something of a bard, a romantic legend persists today, recalling that as

he rowed from Islay's southern shore he sang his 'Praise of Islay':

See afar yon hill Ardmore,
Beating billows wash its shore;
But its beauties bloom no more
For me now far from Islay.

His tack was assigned to the laird, Walter Campbell and his belongings disposed of by Malcolm MacNeil of Ardtallay.

John Johnston of the Tallant distilling family, had meanwhile taken a lease on the other half of the Lagavulin farm, with the approval of Godfrey MacNeil, the tacksman for Callum Kill, and holder of a great many other tacks in Kildalton. MacNeil was well disposed to the family for his daughter Elizabeth had married a Johnston from Corrary where, just across the River Laggan at Island, the MacNeils had their fishing lodge.

Johnston maintained some degree of distilling

activity at Lagavulin until 1835 – his two sons Donald and John were farmer distillers at Laphroaig and Tallant respectively. Johnston died in 1836 and was succeeded in December of that year by Alexander Graham, a Glasgow distillery merchant and owner of the Islay Cellar that supplied Islay malts in Glasgow. It seems that Johnston had got into debt with Graham to the extent that Graham was named as his executor creditor. Graham was no stranger to Islay in any case. His wife Eleanor, was the daughter of Dr Samuel Crawford, the surgeon and resident factor to the laird. Crawford's wife Margaret was the daughter of James Campbell of Ballinaby whose land had been originally held by the Beatons, the surgeons to the Lords of the Isles, and was never a part of the Islay Estate.

A valuation carried out in 1837 by Donald MacDougall clearly shows that two distilleries had been operating at Lagavulin during Johnston's tenancy. 'The Still House (No 2), Tun Room and Malt Barn No 4' were all listed as belonging to the laird Walter Frederick Campbell, as the Ardmore Distillery. The valuation for Lagavulin Distillery itself was £1,103 9s 8d, excluding the farm.

Graham was granted a new lease for the distillery and farm in 1837 for 19 years, but he had no intention of remaining at Lagavulin which he merely saw as a good business opportunity for his sons, Walter and John Crawford Graham. Walter did the distilling until 1848, when Donald Johnston of Laphroaig died. His

Duncan Campbell of Ardmore's inventory of 1784 which clearly records his farming and distilling interests.

Trustees then asked if he would supervise at Laphroaig until Donald's son, Dugald Johnston, was old enough to take over. He did this until November 1855, when he re-entered Lagavulin. After Alexander Graham's death in 1850, John Crawford Graham divided his interests between Lagavulin and the Islay Cellar. His Glasgow business contacts led him to meet the man who was to become his next partner at Lagavulin, James Logan Mackie.

In February 1861, a lease was granted by John Ramsay to the new partners for five years at a rent of £200 for the first year, and £235 per annum for the remainder. At the same time, all the parties agreed to a valuation of the distillery and farm to satisfy themselves as to the extent of their mutual liabilities. This was to become the source of some friction between Ramsay and the Grahams. The survey was carried out by Edward Stewart (Ramsay's nominee) of 364 Argyll Street, Glasgow, and Donald MacDougall (nominated by Walter, John Crawford and their sister Horatia Perry Graham) of Colonsay on July 15th and 16th, 1861. Curiously, the parties did not sign an agreement to the valuation until a few days later. The survey was carried out in two parts, the first dealt with the distillery and the second with the farm, dykes and boundaries. MacDougall had to return to Colonsay after the first survey, leaving Stewart to complete the valuation with the help of a Duncan MacDougall of Port Ellen, a joiner by trade, and sometime employee of John Ramsay. The figures were

The Lagavulin stillhouse in the early 20th century.

The stillhouse today.

worked out in Ramsay's estate office, and were then submitted on unstamped paper.

Nothing was said until the valuation was given to the Graham's solicitor, Mr Faulds, who immediately raised questions. Not only was the distillery valued some £200 less than it had been in 1837, but the Grahams were also found to be owing John Ramsay £330. Faulds then employed an architect, William Spence, whose independent survey of Lagavulin amounted to £1,144. The Grahams remained generally unhappy with the circumstances surrounding the survey, to the point where they felt the presence of Ramsay's joiner MacDougall had been prejudicial. In fact they would have had difficulty casting aspersions on MacDougall's character for he was a devout Christian. He once said of a minister on probation after the death of Rev MacTavish, and who had just delivered a sermon in Kildalton Kirk, ' … it did not appear to me as if he felt that he was in the presence of the Almighty.'

Ramsay decided to take Counsel's opinion in 1862, stating that the Grahams had made additions to the farm without the consent of the laird, and that the distillery buildings had also been 'lessened in number'. The Grahams had indeed made alterations, but it would have been well nigh impossible for the laird to

have remained ignorant of the extent of the alterations. Lagavulin was then one of Islay's largest distilleries having three malt-houses and two kilns which, along with new roads and access, the Grahams had built in 1849. When the corn mill burnt down, they rebuilt it with an undertaking that the estate should pay for the timber and slate – a common enough arrangement in those days. 'In fact Mr Graham and his successors,' claimed Faulds, 'always considered the sums so expended as a fund which to a great extent would be recovered at the expiry of the lease.'

Whether a settlement was ever reached is not recorded. The dispute probably fizzled out as John Crawford Graham got down to business in his new partnership and Horatia moved to the mainland with her husband. Records of Walter Graham's whereabouts also became scarce after 1864. Relations between Ramsay, Graham and Mackie normalised to the extent that new leases were granted over the course of the next 28 years until Mackie's nephew Peter Jeffrey Mackie, who had trained as a distiller at Lagavulin, took over as sole partner in 1889. Just after this date, 'White Horse' was launched by Mackie & Company as a brand which was to enjoy considerable success at home and abroad.

John Ramsay's son Iain maintained a good personal

relationship with Mackie. Both were men of means, but this never stopped them from trying to force the other's hand when business was being conducted, habitually haggling over some minor clause in a lease. By 1902, Mackie was in partnership with Andrew Hair Holm, securing the lease of Lagavulin for £800 per annum (an increase of £110 over the 1889 lease) for 50 years.

Despite the success of 'White Horse', Lagavulin was never entirely divorced from the effects of local disputes. Mackie had, until 1907, held the sales agency of Laphroaig, but suddenly lost it apparently due to an argument concerning the water rights to the Surnaig burn, which had been secured for Lagavulin for some years, and had also been a bone of contention between Dugald Johnston and Walter Graham in 1858. Mackie reacted in characteristic style by deciding to make his own type of Laphroaig whisky, and built a traditional small pot still distillery within the Lagavulin complex. The product of the Malt Mill Distillery did not really do justice to Laphroaig, which should have come as no surprise to Mackie who must have realised that Laphroaig's water had always been drawn from a bog.

At a purely local level Lagavulin was a popular dram in the hotels and public houses of Islay at this time. The distillery sales books of 1913 show transactions on a regular basis to Mrs MacNab of the Islay Hotel, Port Ellen, recording purchases of over 60 gallons of VO (very old) at 21 shillings per gallon almost every month. During and directly after the First World War, the consumption remained around this level.

Lagavulin was one of the distilleries Iain Ramsay was forced to sell off in the early 1920s, although the deal was not entirely straightforward. There were misunderstandings over the sale of the peat lands, which were transferred from the Kildalton Deer Park to the bog just south of Machrie, entailing an increased mileage over which the irascible Mackie argued. Mackie (by then Sir Peter) was very keen to gain more land than Ramsay thought necessary to secure the water rights from the Solan Lochs. Iain Ramsay insisted that water rights should extend from source to

distillery with a margin of land on either side of the burn, but Mackie characteristically haggled for more than he needed. On top of this, some of the correspondence affecting the sale took time to catch up with Mackie during his not infrequent shooting trips in Scotland. The two men agreed to a sum of £16,000 for the distillery, farm, 100 acres of peat lands and the water rights.

Under Sir Peter Mackie, his company had acquired Craigellachie Distillery in 1915, but after his death in 1924 the group's name was changed to White Horse Distillers Limited, taking full advantage of the popularity of its leading brand. The massive amalgamations of the late 1920s saw the company become part of the DCL combine with Lagavulin eventually coming under control of Scottish Malt Distillers (SMD) in 1930. The farm was still going strong at this time and records remain of quarterly expenditure running to £351 from August to September 1929. Items such as 'Fitting corrugated roof on hayshed, McEachern: £54' and 'Waugh, sheep dipper: £20' are clearly detailed.

Only obligatory closures due to war have marred an otherwise continuous production record to the present day, due in no small way to the outstanding quality of Lagavulin as a single malt. The common feature of rationalisation throughout the industry (which was always more evident when carried out by a company the size of DCL) had its way at Lagavulin in the 1970s and 80s. The building of the Port Ellen Maltings made the floor maltings redundant in 1974 and the 'old' Malt Mill Distillery finally succumbed to the economics of the 20th century and was dismantled in 1962. For the next seven years its quaint, coal-fired stills made whisky within the Lagavulin stillhouse to increase output. Finally, they were retired in 1969, and replaced with a pair of traditional Lagavulin pattern stills, all four being converted to internal steam heating at the same time. The old Malt Mill building is now Lagavulin's reception centre where the end-of-cruise ceilidh after the annual Classic Malts Cruise is held.

After the boom period of the 1970s Lagavulin

escaped the SMD closures of 1983, but four jobs were lost out of a workforce of 20 and a four-day week was in operation for some time. Another worrying blow to 'White Horse' came in August 1984 when the DCL announced that they intended closing two bottling plants, both in Scotland – 700 jobs at the VAT 69 plant at South Queensferry and at 'White Horse', Glasgow, were to be lost. The DCL's time as an industry giant was also running out as it was stalked first by Jimmy Gulliver's Argyll Group and then by Guinness under Ernest Saunders. Guinness, having taken over Arthur

Bell in 1985, fought tooth and nail with Gulliver and emerged victorious.

During a period of consolidation, the spirits portfolio of Guinness was renamed United Distillers in 1987 and this led to the creation of the Classic Malts brand. This was a development of the early-80s marketing exercise called The Malt Cellar, which grouped Lagavulin, Talisker, Lochnagar, Linkwood, Rosebank and the vatted Strathconon under one banner. The Classic Malts were chosen on a mix of geographical location and available excellence. Today the brand is headed by Lagavulin and

Lagavulin Distillery

By Port Ellen, Islay, Argyll
PA42 7DZ
Tel: 01496 302400
Fax: 01496 302321
www.malts.com
Owners: Diageo
Manager: Donald Renwick

No distillery could be found amidst a more historical setting than Lagavulin which lies in a fine natural harbour with a clear view of Dunyveg Castle at the entrance. From here 1,000 Islaymen set sail to fight alongside Robert the Bruce at Bannockburn in 1314, and in this bay the Macdonalds maintained their power base as Lords of the Isles until finally driven out by the Campbells three centuries later.

Fortunately the floor maltings escaped demolition in the early 1970s when the final piece was turned, and they

Talisker alongside Oban, Cragganmore, Glenkinchie and Dalwhinnie and is now under the control of Diageo, the company that was formed from the merging of Guinness and Grand Metropolitan in 1997.

For many years the saving grace of the malt distilleries has been the small scale of their operations compared to the huge Lowland grain distilleries which reaped the rewards of Scotch whisky's phenomenal success. New expressions and limited bottlings have maintained interest in the malt and a range of Lagavulin expressions can be found on almost every pub gantry in the UK.

were eventually converted into office accommodation and visitor facilities in the 90s. The whole ambience of this part of the distillery is, I think, almost without peer in the industry. The exterior of the distillery maintains the brilliant crisp, clean appearance with red pagoda kiln roofs that I first encountered almost 20 years ago.

Just past the stillhouse a grey stone slab attached to the side of a building stands as a memorial to Angus Johnston, who died in 1830 at Lagavulin. Although Johnston is buried on Texa island, superstitious boatmen refused to take the headstone across to Johnston's resting place.

The old Malt Mill Distillery, now the reception centre and events space, gives a clue as to the size of a traditional Victorian distillery. In some ways it is regrettable that the old distillery was dismantled, but Peter Mackie's attempt to emulate Laphroaig never really took off.

One of the most enjoyable experiences at Lagavulin is being in the company of Iain McArthur as he takes visitors through a series of casks in the bond. Distiller Donald Renwick has maintained Lagavulin's considerable reputation and ensured that the distillery is actively involved in local community activities including the now traditional Boxing Day dip into the bay from the end of the pier for charity. He is usually the first one in!

LOBSTER BOATS now come and go freely from the bay, but since the instigation of the roll on/roll off ferries to Islay in 1974, the usual means of delivering materials to the distillery by puffer has been stopped. The old DCL-owned puffer *Pibroch* was one of the most frequent visitors to Lagavulin as were many other coasters.

Over the best part of 50 years there were two *Pibrochs* working around the Hebrides. The first coal-fired boat was used by the DCL to service the SMD distilleries in Islay with the occasional summer run up to Talisker in Skye. She became something of a celebrity in 1937 when, within the space of two months, she saved the lives of 22 Fleetwood trawlermen from the *San Sebastian* and *Luneda* which had both come to grief on the treacherous rocks off Islay's southern coast. Not surprisingly she was thereafter known affectionately as the 'Fleetwood Lifeboat'.

By the late 1950s a new boat was required with more efficient diesel power, so in 1957 Scott & Sons of Bowling were commissioned to construct a vessel from plans of G&G Hamilton's *Glen Shira* which had been built the previous year. Her coal-fired predecessor was renamed *Texa* and later *Cumbrae Lass* before being broken up in 1967.

The new vessel plied between Glasgow and Islay until 1974 and a normal week's work for the skipper and crew of five involved taking around 100 tons of malt and grain to Islay, and returning with about 350 hogsheads of malt whisky.

In September 1974, the *Pibroch* was purchased by Glenlight Shipping Company of Glasgow and remained in service until 1983 during which time she had seen use as a tender to the US Navy in the Firth of Clyde. She was then laid up at Yorkhill Quay due to a lack of sufficient work. The future looked a little bleak for the *Pibroch* but rumours of her impending sale

brought enquiries from the United States and Japan – however, Glenlight had no intention of selling their famed asset. Finally, in February 1985, fortune smiled on the puffer when one of the Glenlight's other boats broke down on the way to the Isle of Man, requiring major engine repairs. *The Pibroch* was hurriedly recommissioned and was once more sailing to the Western Isles, back on her home ground.

But the story does not have a happy ending. Glenlight were heavily subsidised by the government to run their fleet and as the writing was on the wall the *Pibroch* was sold in 1988 to Eamonn Mylotte, a Connemara-based skipper. He used the *Pibroch* until 1998 when the Irish authorities forced him to lay her up. Despite strenuous efforts to save her led by Ben Dodd (who restored Barra Head Lighthouse in the 1990s), the *Pibroch* remains a forlorn hulk lying in an unfamiliar harbour, far from her home waters. With a little vision (and a large amount of cash) the *Pibroch* could, and should, be a floating embassy for the whisky industry. The trouble is, time is running out.

Just down the bray from the distillery on the road to Port Ellen sits Surnaig House, once owned by the Ramsay family. For many years until her death in September 1991 Captain Iain Ramsay's daughter-in-law, Freda, maintained the Kildalton Papers which are now housed at the Mitchell Library in Glasgow. This unique collection is one of the great archives for anyone interested in the Kildalton distilleries.

The Pibroch: unloading at Lagavulin in the 1960s (upper); passing Bunnahabhain in 1984 (middle) and at rest at Port Askaig, 1984 (lower).

Laphroaig

IF THE MACDOUGALLS spring to mind when Ardbeg is mentioned, then it is the Johnston family that plays the central role in Laphroaig's establishment and history. Traditionally distillers from Tallant, they were already represented at Lagavulin by John Johnston when his son Donald set up in Laphroaig around 1826 on ground belonging to the Torradale croft which was occupied by his cousin, yet another Johnston. Within 10 years Laphroaig was joined by another distillery on part of the Ardenistiel farm tack leased from Walter Frederick Campbell by James and Andrew Gairdner in 1835. The Gairdners acted as financiers and put the Ardenistiel distillery (it was also referred to as the 'Islay' and 'Kildalton' distillery) in the capable hands of James and Andrew Stein of the noted Clackmannan distilling family. The two concerns existed side by side and initially did not appear to suffer from their proximity.

In 1846 Andrew Stein died of fever, which is now thought to have been malarial in nature, and his brother moved to Port Ellen Distillery to act as manager and factor to his cousin John Ramsay, having married John's sister Margaret. Ardenistiel was then assigned by the Gairdners in 1847 to John Morrison, who had been an unsuccessful manager in his stay at Port Ellen between 1826 and 1833, but was effectively being given a second chance. In June 1847, Donald Johnston died, popularly believed to have drowned in a pot of his own burnt ale. This is not quite as pleasant a way to die as one might first think. In April of the following year an Excise officer at Port Ellen Distillery fell into a tank of spent wash immersing himself 'in the boiling liquor to the upper part of both thighs and was so severely scalded as to baffle every medical attention to save his life.'

Donald's eldest son Dugald, then in his minority, became heir to Laphroaig. Donald's trustees were named as Peter MacIntyre, tenant in Ballynaughton-more farm and John Johnston of Tallant, Donald's brother. Both men recognised the need for a knowledgeable distiller to take over the day-to-day running of Laphroaig. They installed Walter Graham (who had followed Donald's father in 1836 as distiller at Lagavulin) soon after Donald's death and also

renegotiated the lease with the new laird, James Morrison, in February 1854.

After James Stein withdrew from Ardenistiel, John Morrison was once more unable to make a go of it, and he signed it over to William Hunter and John Ferguson Sharpe in 1848. He continued, however, to hold the licence and distil there until May 1851, when the Excise noted thankfully that 'Mr Morrison has paid up all his excise duties long ago and does not intend to take out another licence.' It seems that Morrison was never destined to be a distiller – when James Morrison visited Ardenistiel in 1848 prior to his purchase of Islay, he discovered that his namesake had 2,000 pigs grazing on Texa island!

Typically, John Morrison had responded somewhat too enthusiastically to a brilliant suggestion by Walter Frederick Campbell that pigs might be raised on the distillery farms and fed on draff. The hams could then be smoked in the kilns during the silent season and despatched by sea to the mainland. Sadly, his own bankruptcy and the advent of the railways system on the mainland put paid to Campbell's inspiration. By the end of 1852, Hunter and Sharpe realised they had backed the wrong horse and assigned 'all and whole of the said distillery called the Kildalton Distillery … and the right of water from the Surnaig Burn … ' to Robert Salmond, manager of the City and Glasgow Bank. John Morrison had by now returned to Glasgow and is recorded as being in the Glenpatrick Distillery in the 1860s, where predictably, he was to be finally bankrupted.

The new laird of Kildalton, John Ramsay, was becoming increasingly impatient with the way things were going at Ardenistiel, but decided to give one last chance to William and Andrew Hunter, granting a lease in their favour in 1859 for 19 years.

In 1858 Dugald Johnston was assigned the land lease of Laphroaig by his father's trustees, and Walter Graham claimed to have 'nearly doubled the capabilities of Laphroaig's distillery since 1848.' Dugald Johnston gradually became more involved with the distilling, but had to withstand the quarrelling of his sisters, Mary, Isabella (who married Dugald's cousin, Alexander Johnston of Tallant), Margaret and Ann, all of whom disputed the assignation. Walter Graham returned to Lagavulin, but continued to live in Ardenistiel House having taken out 19-year leases in 1852 on the farm, Texa island, and also on the Ardelistry farm for 14 years from 1850.

When Dugald finally took over the reins at Laphroaig he is reputed to have held Walter Graham responsible for not having secured the water rights to the Surnaig burn which already supplied the Ardenistiel distillery and which John Morrison had been granted by the Reverend Archibald MacTavish, as the burn ran through his glebe. There is almost certainly more to the story than meets the eye, for Laphroaig's water supply had always been the bog to the north of the public road in any case, and Walter Graham was married to MacTavish's daughter, Elizabeth. The outcome of the quarrel was that Dugald withdrew Laphroaig from sale in the Islay Cellar in Glasgow, which was owned by the Grahams.

After first entering John Cassels in 1852 as the distiller in Ardenistiel, William Hunter took over but gave up the struggle sometime in the 1860s having rarely achieved full production. When Port Ellen was turning over ten washbacks a week, producing 115,000 gallons (552,100 litres) of spirit a year, Ardenistiel managed only 33,000 gallons (149,820 litres) – about half the distillery's potential output. John Ramsay finally decided enough was enough and had the place thrown in with Laphroaig, along with the manager's house which was then used by the resident Excise officer.

Dugald Johnston continued to manage the distillery with Isabella's husband, Alexander Johnston of Tallant, playing an increasing role in the operation before

THE JOHNSTONS OF TALLANT AND LAPHROAIG

Showing how the ownership of Laphroaig moved from the Laphroaig branch of the family to the Tallant branch following the death of Sandy Johnston in 1907 and the transferral of the lease to Sandy's sisters Catherine and Isabella and his nephew, John Johnston Hunter Johnston.

John Johnston of Tallant & Lagavulin d. 1836

John Johnston of Tallant — Donald Johnston of Laphroaig d. 1847

| ? | Isabella 1843-1927 | Catherine 1846-1926 | Alexander d. 1907 | — m — | Isabella d. c1905 | Mary | Margaret (m.Campbell) | Anne (m. Brandon) | Dugald d. 1877 |

John Johnston Hunter Johnston

m
William Stevenson Hunter 1848-1919

Ian William Hunter d. 1954

m
Alexander Campbell

Isabella

Sandy Johnston and his wife Isabella (upper left); Catherine Johnston (lower left); William Stevenson Hunter and his wife Isabella (upper centre); Ian William Hunter (upper right and lower)

Laphroaig Distillery staff, 1934. Ian Hunter sits atop the cask in the centre with Iain Ramsay on his left.
On the far right is the demure secretary Bessie Williamson, who fell heir to Laphroaig after Hunter's death.

Dugald died in January 1877. At Lagavulin, Walter's brother, John Crawford Graham was in partnership with James Logan Mackie. These two men, together with Colin Hay of Ardbeg were named as Dugald's trustees, maintaining this position over the course of the next 10 years while Alexander remained in charge of the distillery.

In 1887, the Trustees renounced the lease in favour of John Ramsay and new leases were negotiated and granted to Isabella, her husband Alexander, her sister Mary (by then married to an Alexander Campbell, whose exact whereabouts were always in doubt) and their daughter Isabella Campbell. At the same time they 'agreed to pay Mrs Margaret Johnston, or Campbell, sister of the said Dugald Johnston, the sum of £300 Sterling, and to the family of Mrs Ann Johnston or Brandon, now deceased, also a sister of the said Dugald Johnston, the sum of £100 Sterling … ' In

effect they had bought out their interests in the distillery. The new leases were for the distillery, with water rights to the Surnaig burn along with peatlands, the farm, Texa Island and Torrodale Park, and the buildings which belonged to the Ardenistiel distillery. In all, a quite considerable holding for the time.

In 1904 Alexander Johnston negotiated new leases for the farm and the distillery for a further 15 years, but his wife Isabella died shortly afterwards and his sister Catherine arrived to housekeep for him. She did not concern herself solely with domestic affairs, and must have been a woman far removed from the silk and lace ladies of Edwardian drawing room melodrama, for when Alexander died in 1907 she promptly took over the running of the distillery. This fact was not lost on Alexander's trustees, the Edinburgh Writers and Solicitors, Menzies, Bruce-Low and Thomson who were soon to find out how formidable she was when they informed her that Alexander had made more than one will.

Apparently Alexander had made two or three wills, the last of which benefited his cousin and sister-in-law, Mary and her daughter, Isabella Campbell, a great deal more than Catherine thought proper. The second last will was more to Catherine's liking since it favoured herself, her sister Isabella Hunter and their nephew John Johnston Hunter alone. Naturally, she informed the trustees that this was the one that would be executed. A letter from Menzies, Bruce-Low and Thomson to Ian Ramsay's factor Peter Reid, dated August 12th 1907 states that 'after providing for a few small legacies under Mr Johnston's will, his sister, Miss Catherine Johnston, is sole beneficiary, so that the whole plant and stock-in-trade at Laphroaig falls to her.' The trustees then asked Iain Ramsay to renew the leases in the beneficiaries' favour. Whether he was suspicious or just merely curious is not recorded, but he seems to have wanted an explanation as to why the lease should include Isabella. The trustees came clean,

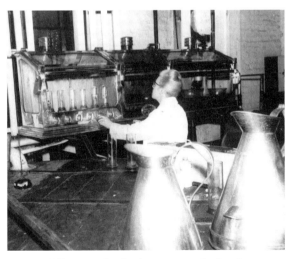

Bessie Willamson checks the spirit at the Laphroaig spirit safe.

and in the couched language of a law firm that had, strictly speaking, not been playing ball, they replied to Peter Reid on August 26th:

As regards Mrs Hunter being one of the tenants, along with Miss Johnston and Mr Hunter Johnston, we have to say it will be a disappointment to all three if Mrs Hunter is not one of the tenants. We feel that in putting her name before Mr Ramsay, we did not give a sufficient explanation of her position in relation to the late Mr Johnston's estate; and accordingly we can appreciate the reasonableness of Mr Ramsay entertaining a doubt as to why she should have been brought forward at all. We are now desired to inform you that, by arrangement among Miss Johnston, Mr Hunter Johnston, and Mrs Hunter, the estate of the late Mr Johnston is not to be divided in accordance with the latest date of his Wills, and that effect is to be given to a great extent to an earlier Will, which was prepared for Mr Johnston by the present writer, under which Will, after providing for certain legacies, including substantial legacies to Miss Johnston, Mrs Hunter, and Mr Hunter Johnston, the residue was to be divided equally among these three. Miss Johnston was good enough to be the first to suggest a departure from the terms of the latest Will; and an Agreement on the subject was signed shortly after Mr Johnston's death. Under this agreement Mrs Hunter will receive a legacy of £1,100, and, over and above that, one third of the ultimate residue.

We may say that our own feeling was that, when we wrote you first proposing the granting of the new Lease, we ought, in justice to Mrs Hunter, to have given you the above explanation; and that we withheld it only in deference to the wishes of Mr Johnston's relatives, who, not unnaturally, were anxious that, if possible, knowledge of their arrangement should be kept to those immediately concerned. They wished to avoid any possibility of the affairs of the late Mr Johnston, and the

The boiler installed in 1924 and replaced in 1955 with a similar item that was floated in from the bay.

all concerned that she should be a tenant. So far as her circumstances are concerned, we think the interest she has in her brother's estate sufficiently warrants her becoming one of the tenants.

Satisfied, but no doubt a little amused by the whole affair, Iain Ramsay did grant a lease to John Johnston Hunter Johnston and his two aunts. Catherine thus followed the MacDougall sisters of Ardbeg and Lucy Ramsay of Port Ellen as one of the first legal lady distillers in Scotland (not forgetting their illicit distilling female counterparts in Campbeltown). But control of Laphroaig had passed into the hands of the Tallant branch of the family and this precipitated much litigation from Alexander's excluded in-laws which forced John to give up the lease and have a new one issued to himself, Catherine, Isabella and her husband William Stevenson Hunter. Their son, Ian William Hunter was to become the central figure in the development and modernisation of Laphroaig from 1910 onwards. By the time of his father's death in 1919, he had assumed his father's place in the partnership and became sole partner after the deaths of his aunt Catherine in 1926, and his mother the next year. By 1924, he had purchased the distillery, Texa Island, and Ardenistiel House from Capt Iain Ramsay, remaining sole proprietor until his death in 1954.

Laphroaig was imported legally into the United States during prohibition as a medicinal spirit thanks to its conveniently ambiguous character. However, these levels of consumption were not high enough to satisfy Ian Hunter, for he had also lost another valuable overseas market due to prohibition, namely, Norway. Having increased capacity from two to four stills in 1923, he continued to sink every last penny into Laphroaig in the belief that things could only get better. The repeal of prohibition in 1933 amply rewarded Hunter's foresight.

Around this time a young Glasgow girl, Bessie Williamson, had just graduated and answered an

Wills made by him, being a matter of general discussion. They thought too, that mention of the arrangement might cause a little heartburning on the part of the other relatives of the deceased. For the reasons we have indicated, Mr Ramsay and you will be so good as to receive in confidence the information we have now given.

In view of what we have said, we hope Mr Ramsay will see his way to allow Mrs Hunter to be one of the tenants. The intention has been that she, like her sister and nephew, should leave her share of the estate in the business. Her interest would therefore be a substantial one. It would be for the advantage and convenience of advertisement placed by Hunter for a temporary shorthand typist. Having just taken a business training course, she was hired to help out at the distillery, proving to be so efficient that Hunter offered her the secretary's job on a permanent basis. She could not have suspected then that should would one day rise to the same position that Catherine Johnston had held so tenaciously.

Hunter regained his markets in Scandinavia and began an ambitious promotional tour of the United States before the outbreak of World War II. He first made a call on Thomas Sherriff in Jamaica who had been involved in Bowmore Distillery until 1922, and was looking after his sugar plantations and rum distillery. Hunter suffered a slight stroke and was unable to continue the tour so, facing a great loss in potential trade, he cabled Bessie Williamson to join him in Jamaica where he briefed her on his full itinerary. She thus became one of the first promoters of malt whisky on the other side of the Atlantic. Her successful tour was the first of several visits including one to the New York Trade Fair in June 1969 as the representative of the Scotch Whisky Association (SWA).

The importance of Scotch whisky during the war years as a valuable dollar earner was recognised by Ian Hunter but his business drained his health until he was confined to a wheelchair. To safeguard Laphroaig he formed a private company in partnership with his lawyer and accountant, with Bessie Williamson as Company Secretary. She became the driving force at the distillery and was involved in all aspects of management from the malt-house to the bonds.

Ian Hunter died at Laphroaig on August 28th 1954 with no heirs. He left not only his entire personal property but also the distillery and the company to Bessie Williamson. She gained a great deal of recognition in the 1950s and 60s as Scotland's 'first lady distiller', which as we now know was not true, but did no harm to Laphroaig's sales or to the cachet of the distillery.

In 1962 the sale of 51% of the business was negotiated with Long John Distillers Limited, the subsidiary of the Seager Evans group. The distillery was expanded in 1968 with the addition of another pair of stills, but the working practices were still very much a thing of the past ' … we do it this way, because that is the way we have always done it.' Bessie, by then Mrs Wishart Campbell, was to remain as the nominal Managing Director until 1972 before retiring to Ardenistiel House. In 1970 she agreed the sale of the rest of the business for £300,000 (in instalments) to the newly-formed Long John International, which was a subsidiary of the American corporation, Schenley of

An old-fashioned coal-fired puffer unloading at Laphroaig in the 1930s.

Cincinnati. Given that Long John's profits were then standing at £900,000 per annum, this could be considered something of a premium price.

But before Bessie departed from the day-to-day management of Laphroaig, Long John knew that they had to have someone in charge who would not be afraid to ring the changes. Laphroaig was languishing and living off its laurels, and the distillery was in dire need of capital investment and modern working practices. In January 1970, John McDougall was a 28-year-old distiller working for William Grant & Sons as manager of Balvenie Distillery on Speyside. Over a dram at the home of Duncan McGregor, production

director of Long John Distillers, near Tormore Distillery, whilst watching Wales beat Scotland 9-3 in the Home Nations rugby international, John was offered the job of taking over at Laphroaig. Although initially reluctant to agree, he was offered £2000 per annum with a house and company car thrown in. He agreed and arrived in Islay in April 1970 with his wife Kay. He was not impressed with what he found.

Despite Bessie's presence at Laphroaig, the housekeeping had been poor and a full programme of renovation, rebuilding and general tidying up was put in place. The yields, which stood at 2.54 gallons per bushel when John arrived, were gradually improved to 2.75, which was quite an achievement for a heavily peated malt. Production was also increased from 360,000 to 430,000 proof gallons per annum (1.634 to 1.952 million litres) and the water source was strengthened with the building of a new dam that reserved five million gallons of water. At the same time, the tunroom capacity was doubled and another wash still installed.

Another addition created a change in the Laphroaig style which was not as welcome. John was unable to convince his American masters that a new spirit still they wanted installed in 1972 would lead to an alteration in the character of the distillate. Instead of adding two new stills

Laphroaig Distillery

Laphroaig Distillery
By Port Ellen, Islay, Argyll
PA42 7DU
Tel: 01496 302418
Fax: 01496 302496
www.laphroaig.com
Owners: Allied Distillers
Manager: Robin Shields

The turning point for Laphroaig came after Bessie Willamson retired in 1972 and John McDougall arrived to bring the distillery up to speed. After John had reshaped production, Denis Nicol took over and was succeeded by Murdo Reed who was in charge at the time of my original visit in 1984. Nothing was too much trouble for him. He organised the peat cutters for the photographers (they weren't due to start for another week and one of them, Michael Heads, is now in charge at Jura), conducted an in-depth tour and took time to talk about Laphroaig over a dram in his office.

These elements of care and hospitality were still evident in September 1998 when I visited again in order identical to the three in existence, another was added exactly twice the size as the smaller type. An additional boiler, to double the steam-raising capability, was also installed and the overall effect of all these developments was that the production output rose to 700,000 proof gallons per annum (3.178 million litres). But the end-result was that the traditional heavy, peaty, oily, smoky, phenolic, iodine-like Laphroaig was no longer made and a more emasculated product emerged. Although home trade bottling strength remained at 43% for some years it was eventually reduced to 40% as well.

John's work at Laphroaig did not go unrewarded and he was promoted within the company by taking over at Tormore in April 1974, becoming General Manager of Distilleries a few years later. He was succeeded at Laphroaig by Denis Nicol who stayed until the late 70s and then Murdo Reed arrived. At the time of my first visit in 1984 Murdo had overseen the renovation of the stillhouse once more, as all seven stills were rotated 180° and a new roof put in place. The whole operation was done without loss to production. Murdo was promoted to manager at Tormore and was followed for a short period by Colin Ross (now at Ben Nevis Distillery) before Iain Henderson arrived in

June 1989.

But even by the mid-1970s the days of Laphroaig as a privately-owned, remote island distillery had gone. As part of an American corporation with no great degree of emotional attachment to it, it was always likely to be the subject of a change of ownership and so it proved to be. In 1975 the brewers Whitbread acquired Long John International Ltd from Schenley for £18.5m and this was to lead to the eventual purchase in January 1990 by Allied-Lyons PLC of the spirits portfolio of Whitbread for £545m in cash.

Under Allied Distillers ownership (the subsidiary of Allied-Lyons PLC) and Iain Henderson's management Laphroaig went from strength to strength. The Prince of Wales even stated that Laphroaig was the 'best whisky in the world' and over 100,000 enthusiasts from all parts of the globe are 'Friends of Laphroaig'. Each one of them can visit the distillery and receive a free dram in lieu of the rental the distillery owes them for a square foot of peat bog 'sold' to them when they first purchased a bottle of Laphroaig and responded to this ingenious promotion. The interaction between the Friends and Laphroaig can be experienced on the Laphroaig website which sets a high standard for other distilleries to match.

to prepare an article on the distillery for the first issue of *Whisky* Magazine, published in November that year. Iain Henderson, whom I had first encountered at Bladnoch in 1987 when preparing a BBC Radio Scotland broadcast on Alfred Barnard, was clearly continuing in the same vein. Iain has rightly been credited with the modern face of Laphroaig and prior to his retirement in December 2002 had done a huge amount to promote the brand and the island around the world. Some who came before him worked under very different conditions, such as John McDougall, turning the distillery into a modern and efficient plant. Some hard decisions had to be made but he managed to maintain cordial relations with the Ileachs and still returns to Islay today.

Arguably the most famous island malt of all, Laphroaig's situation does not disappoint and gives as much pleasure to the eye as its dram does to the palate. Sheltered in a small cove visited by otters and swans, the layout still resembles the distillery when it was rebuilt in the 1870s.

If you were lucky enough to visit during Islay's Whisky Festival in May 2002, you would have seen Iain in his element conducting tours that had been booked out well in advance with his usual fastidiousness and good humour. His successor will have a hard act to follow but Robin Shields, who arrived on the 24th March 2003, will know exactly which direction Laphroaig is heading.

Port Ellen

ANY VISITOR to Islay about to disembark at Port Askaig will be struck by the bleak hills and deep glens behind McArthur's Head at the mouth of the Sound of Islay. This solitary region holds the attention of the unfamiliar traveller from many miles distant until the ferry is ready to berth. It displays many of those features for which much of Islay is famous – dark, sombre corries amongst high rolling hills commanding views to Kintyre with a total lack of human habitation. The development of the distillery at Port Ellen owes much to the determination of a young midland Scot who was forced to make landfall near McArthur's Head in 1833 and then make his way overland to Port Ellen.

John Ramsay was then only 18 and the nephew of the Procurator Fiscal of Clackmannan, Ebenezer Ramsay, who was in charge of the extensive distilling interests that the family fostered around Alloa. John's cousin, John Morrison, had been placed in charge of the distillery which had been developed from a malt

mill erected by Alexander Kerr MacKay in 1825 with Walter Frederick Campbell's approval and converted during the next few years into a distillery.

These formative years show how complicated the lease arrangements were in those days. MacKay held the ground lease for the distillery, while the lease for the buildings was held by Major James Adair of Dumfries and Glasgow, who in turn sub-let to John Morrison and his associates, George MacLennan and Patrick Thomson. Despite this curious situation, it was MacKay who appears to have held the reins, for when £300 was granted by Adair in 1831 for 'improvements and additions to Port Ellen Distillery and its utensils' it was MacKay who had requested the aid on Morrison's behalf. Only when MacKay died in 1833 did Adair finally gain complete control by purchasing the ground lease from MacKay's assignee Michael Rowand Ronald.

Things did not go well at Port Ellen under John Morrison's management and Ebenezer despatched his

The Port Ellen pontoons which were opened in July 2002 by Sir Chay Blyth.

son Eben to report back, but receiving no word from him he started John Ramsay on his precarious journey to finally sort things out. His uninspiring landing near Gleann Choiredail left him with a 12-mile (19-km) hike guided only by a compass and a wealth of good common sense. Unknown to him, Eben was at that moment sailing for the mainland on the very winds that had forced John onto the opposite side of the island.

Completing the last few miles on a pony lent to him by the MacDougalls of Arivochallum, he arrived at Port Ellen to learn from John Morrison that Eben was going to report to his father that the distillery was unworkable. This, John was soon to realise, was not the case and he informed his uncle that the operation had a future in the right hands. With the timely arrival of his elder brother, Thomas, from new Brunswick, a new partnership was formed whereby Morrison was to enter the Glasgow office to take charge of sales. Thomas would manage grain supplies and John, after training as a distiller under Morrison's brother James in Alloa, was to run the distillery at an annual salary of £150. Eben meanwhile, clearly had had enough of the whole affair, and disappeared to New Orleans, where

his uncle James was a merchant.

The arrangement, however, was unsuccessful from the start. Thomas Ramsay soon realised that John Morrison was an impossible partner and quit, following Eben across the Atlantic where it is believed he lost his life in the Mexican War of 1836-7. Although barely in his 20s, John Ramsay was already creating very favourable impressions with the many businessmen he dealt with in Glasgow and Islay. Adair, who had lost a leg at Waterloo in the year of John's birth, allowed him free rein to establish his business. Within a year, Ebenezer's second son, and John Ramsay's cousin, also called Thomas, joined the partnership to the exclusion of the unfortunate John Morrison who in 1837 was eventually to take over from his cousin James Stein in Ardenistiel Distillery at Laphroaig.

Walter Frederick Campbell was so impressed with the young Lowlander that he asked him to look into his personal affairs that were in some disarray. Ramsay confirmed the worst and moved to take a proactive part in Campbell's dealings. He became a business partner of the laird's ensuring that Campbell's steamer services to the mainland (which had been instituted with great

Distillery staff, 1895.

foresight in the late 1820s) were properly maintained and managed and their business relationship was to develop further over the years.

Under Ramsay's management the distillery gradually expanded with a second duty free warehouse being added in 1839 due to his 'present increased business'. He was, however, only a tenant and after Adair died in 1840 the leases became vacant and the distillery was put up for sale. John Ramsay badly needed the leases if he was to consolidate his business interests in Port Ellen, but legally the distillery and the leases were up

for auction to the highest bidder. Alexander Craig of Wadeston Mills, Glasgow entered the highest bid of £1,950 but was unable to secure the sale because Walter Frederick Campbell exercised his right of pre-emption at the expiry of the leases and matched Craig's bid, thus assuring his partner Ramsay the purchase of the distillery, and a new lease. At the age of 25, Ramsay had gained the first of his Kildalton Distilleries. Once Ramsay had repaid Campbell he took out leases on two neighbouring farms at Cornabus and Kilnaughton, finally settling in Port Ellen as farmer and distiller.

The distillery in 1935.

By 1842, his inventory showed 7,399 gallons (33,590 litres) of whisky in bond worth £1,479 16s out of a whole stock in hand including barley, bere, peats, coals, and feints amounting to £4,193 19s 8d. A letter dated 8th April 1844 from Walter Campbell to John Ramsay shows the depth of their relationship. In it Campbell not only reveals his serious health problems to Ramsay, but also exhorts him to take advantage of the fact that Queen Victoria was purchasing Port Ellen whisky for Her Majesty's Cellar to create greater demand for the product.

Much of his early business success was due to trade with North America by direct export from Port Ellen. As the distiller's spokesman, he actively sought the lifting of restrictions in 1848 which allowed spirits to be exported in casks exceeding 80 gallons capacity and the right to store whisky in bond, duty free, for export. The Port Ellen warehouses are not only some of the earliest constructed for this purpose, but are reputed to be amongst the best.

By this time his sister Margaret had joined him at Cornabus farm and married James Stein who had been managing Ardenistiel Distillery with his brother Andrew. Stein became Ramsay's factor and distillery manager, effectively freeing him to attend to his affairs in Glasgow where he imported sherry and Madeira wine, and coincidentally had a house in Madeira Court. Together they were to refine the spirit safe that had been invented in the early 1820s by Septimus Fox and adopted by the Excise after the Act of 1823.

Just as Walter Frederick Campbell's estate was about to collapse, so John Ramsay's grew, largely due to fortuitous inheritance and astute management on his part. He was gifted with a great feel for the land and became one of Islay's leading agriculturists, voicing his opinions on farming matters as a regular contributor to the *Glasgow Herald*. Campbell sought and took heed of Ramsay's advice in a last ditch effort to sort out the affairs of his badly managed estate, but as Joseph Mitchell, one of Thomas Telford's roving engineers, observed around this time, 'unfortunately Mr Campbell was no man of business.' In fairness, the

laird had become the victim of circumstances far outwith his control, and it was too late for John Ramsay's good judgement and sound business advice to save him. On the 2nd December 1847 Campbell finally agreed to sequestration when the rental arrears owed to his estate stood at £32,095. Personal debt, heritable bonds and bank loans amounted to over £750,000 and the income from his estates was insufficient to pay even the interest on his loans. His estates were put up for sale in November 1848 with an asking price of £540,000 for his lands on Islay.

No buyer was forthcoming and, until August 1853, the entire estate was held in trust under his son John Francis Campbell and John Ramsay; the creditors being represented by James Brown, an Edinburgh accountant, during this period. The sale prospectus fulsomely extolled the nature of the estate that, 'can nowhere be excelled'.

Despite the uncertainty of the estate's future, life and work went on. In particular, Campbell and Ramsay's steam packet company had been gradually evolving. In 1846 the wooden-hulled *Modern Athens* had been commissioned on the Glasgow to Islay route and she was followed in 1849 by the first *Islay* which was part-owned by some of the other island distillers including the Mutters of Bowmore, the Grahams of Lagavulin and Ardbeg's financier, Thomas Buchanan. (The *Islay* was nearly wrecked in 1866 and *Islay II* replaced her in 1867.)

In July 1849, an English merchant James Morrison, the son of a Scots cattle drover who had settled in Wiltshire (a man who was regarded as one of the richest 'commoners' in England) had visited Islay with some of his family. He was clearly as canny as his Scots ancestors because it was some four years later that he eventually offered, through the office of his son Charles, £451,000 in a public sale of the estate. The Islay estate finally had a new laird and he was immediately drawn into the steam packet company's future. One of the results of Walter Frederick Campbell's sequestration had been the passing of control of the *Islay* to John Ramsay who then persuaded Charles Morrison to become a half-owner in the business after Ramsay had secured complete ownership of the vessel in 1857 for the sum of £944 from the other shareholders.

In the 1860s Morrison took overall control after Ramsay transferred his shares in the vessel to him because of fears that he might lose his parliamentary seat over the issue of the company receiving a £150 annual subsidy from the Royal Mail for carrying the mails on the vessel. But Ramsay continued to manage the business 'without loss' and ensured that sea-borne trade and passenger traffic between Port Ellen, Glasgow, Tarbert, Port Rush, Stornoway and other points in between, was as regular as the weather allowed. Eventually the business was sold to David Hutcheson & Company (one of the forerunners of Caledonian MacBrayne) in 1876.

Ramsay wasted no time in asking Charles Morrison to become a part-owner in the cargo screw-steamer, *The City of Worcester*, which began to ply between Islay and Glasgow in 1853 servicing Port Ellen and Ardbeg. The other part-owner, once again, was Thomas Buchanan, Ardbeg's financial backer.

When James Morrison had bought the Islay estate, Ramsay had cannily negotiated the future purchase of the Kildalton portion for the sum of £82,265 and so in 1855 Ramsay became owner and landlord of Laphroaig, Ardenistiel, Lagavulin and Ardbeg distilleries with all the associated farms, pastures and distillery villages. Ramsay ensured that the Kildalton Distillery owners enjoyed long leases and had properly secured water rights, something that was frequently overlooked in those days. Through the influence of his first wife, Eliza, Ardbeg gained a school which was completed after her death in 1864 and Ramsay ensured that the teacher's salary was met, even though he was not directly responsible for it.

Ramsay's other interests included the instigation of the construction of new roads throughout Kildalton. His distilling business in Port Ellen no longer required his full-time attention which he now gave to politics and public service. When it became apparent to him that there was insufficient food grown on the island to feed all of his tenants, he encouraged the more able amongst them to emigrate to Canada. The manner in which this was carried out says a great deal for his humanity and common sense and many of the Islay families crossed the Atlantic at his expense to build new futures in Canada's eastern provinces. He visited them in 1870 and was pleased to see them well established, as his granddaughter-in-law, the late Freda

Port Ellen Distillery when it was last active in the early 1980s.

Ramsay of Kildalton, recorded 100 years later:

All through Huronia and the townships north-east of Lake Simcoe it is possible to see fine farms, with the delightful houses which succeeded the log cabins, still occupied by descendants of the men and women with whom John Ramsay talked during his visit. Many of the younger generations have spread across the length and breadth of North America and the prosperity and happiness they have created for themselves is the finest memorial John Ramsay could have wished.

The Glasgow end of the business had been managed by John Morrison, followed by James Richardson and then W P Lowrie, who left in 1869 to start up on his own, successfully blending and bottling Scotch whisky in bond. Although he was later erroneously credited for having initiated these practices in Scotland, he did introduce some innovation into the production and marketing of Scotch which remain with us today. He was the first to pre-treat casks when a scarcity of sherry butts for fillings occurred in the late 19th century and he installed a large bottling plant at his works in Washington Street, Glasgow (which now houses the offices of this book's publishers) which effectively made his operation self-contained.

Three years before his death in 1892 John Ramsay granted a lease to his second wife Lucy for the land on the seaward side of the distillery. Here she built four villas – one for herself (should her daughter ever marry), and the others for distillery and excise workers. Her involvement in the distillery deepened when Ramsay died at Kildalton House on January 24th 1892, aged 77 and the day-to-day running of the business passed to her. In September of that year a special meeting was convened to determine 'payments to Mrs Ramsay for spirits at Port Ellen, sold during John Ramsay's lifetime but not delivered' which stood at 160,287 gallons (727,700 litres) as of the end of June, 1892. The valuators were A W Robertson of Robertson and Baxter, the Glasgow whisky brokers, and W P Lowrie and between them they fixed the price of the peats, feints, malt and coals taken over by Mrs Ramsay as follows:

1,200 *carts of peats at 2s a cart.*
359 *gallons feints at 1s per proof gallon.*
400 *bushels of Malt at 25s a quarter.*
25 *tons coals at 10s a ton.*

At the same time it was decided that John Ramsay's grand-nephew and manager, J R Stein, would leave the firm no later than September 30th with a final pay cheque for £16 13s 4d.

An eminently practical woman, who had never favoured Stein, Lucy Ramsay then took over with a Mr Osborne as manager until her death in 1905. (The distillery had remained part of John Ramsay's estate until just after the turn of the century.) Her son Iain Ramsay, aged 27, then took over the business while his mother's capital in the plant was inherited by his sister, Miss Lucy. From this point on Iain Ramsay was to struggle as best he could to keep the distillery business on a sound footing, and he was forced to find a business partner in 1912, when his sister decided to lift her capital from the business to buy an estate on the mainland. At that time, he was employing Malcolm MacIntyre of Train & MacIntyre Limited, as a trainee distiller and agreed to take him in just as the Great War loomed.

Ramsay and MacIntyre both joined up but only Ramsay survived, returning as an invalided captain to find his business in want of capital, and his markets rapidly receding due to the effects of war and the introduction of prohibition in America. He was in bad health, his stored household effects had all been destroyed in a Zeppelin raid and he was forced to sell off his assets and parts of his estate in order to maintain the remainder.

W P Lowrie had fared better and his firm was now owned by James Buchanan & Company Limited since Lowrie's retirement in 1906. For years Lowrie had acted as Buchanan's main supplier and no doubt his intimate knowledge of Port Ellen Distillery may have moved Buchanan to acquire the distillery and its assets in partnership with John Dewar & Sons Limited in 1920 as the Port Ellen Distillery Company Limited.

An aerial view of the distillery and maltings.

After the final merging of Buchanan-Dewar with the DCL in 1925, Port Ellen was absorbed into the group until the company was voluntarily liquidated two years later as part of the DCL's rationalisation programme – due largely to the effects of the Depression. The assets were then acquired by John Dewar & Son Limited and W P Lowrie & Company Limited before being finally transferred to SMD in 1930. At this time the DCL and its subsidiaries were taking over the largest and finest stocks of maturing whisky anywhere in Scotland and although Port Ellen was officially closed in 1930 due to the Depression and general economic climate, there can be no doubt that the distillery possessed an extensive stock in bond. At that time there was enough whisky warehoused in Port Ellen to last 40 years, and the more cynical observers will remind you that it was fully 37 years before the distillery came on stream again.

In order 'to meet the needs of its blending companies,' the Distillers Company Limited decided to bring Port Ellen 'back into production' in the mid-1960s. The industry in general was expanding around this time with Charles Mackinlay's Jura Distillery once more in production and a great deal of development being carried out in the Highlands, enabling the malt sector to double its output during the decade.

Port Ellen did become an extremely efficient distillery after a rebuild that was completed in April 1967. The cost ran to approximately £400,000 with major improvements to the malt barns, steeps and kilns and other substantial parts of the plant and process. Although some of the original buildings were retained, in 1973 the character of the shore-side site was again changed when the vast industrial maltings were erected. Capable of producing 400 tonnes of malted barley each week, the maltings initially supplied only the three SMD distilleries on Islay making their own floor maltings redundant. But the curious spectacle of loads of malt being trucked the short distance around the block to Port Ellen Distillery ceased in May 1983 when it was one of the 11 SMD distilleries closed by the DCL in their efforts to cut back production. Why?

At the time of closure the DCL stated that Port Ellen's closure was 'part of the measures taken by Scottish Malt Distillers to reduce output in order to bring the level of maturing stock into line with the anticipated level of future sales.' In other words it was the old problem of over-capacity.

There is no doubt that at the time the DCL had to make some very difficult decisions in both human and economic terms, but these are naturally exacerbated in an island community. The decision to close Port Ellen did not appear to have been taken with this in mind. Having decided on the requirement for a Hebridean closure, Port Ellen may well have been chosen because of the better reputation of Caol Ila, Lagavulin and Talisker within the blending trade, notwithstanding the popularity of the last two as single malts.

Although then renowned as a company insensitive to criticism, the DCL must have taken note of the unfavourable press that Highland Distilleries received in March 1982 when Bunnahabhain was closed and almost the entire community around the distillery was made redundant. On all counts, Port Ellen was the most likely candidate. In a town with an unemployment rate of 20 per cent, the effects were spelt out in the local paper, the *Ileach* in terms which the board of the DCL may not have fully appreciated at the time:

There will be less draff so the farmers will suffer as will Willie Currie's haulage business. Mundell's transport will lose half a day's work involved in taking malt from maltings to distillery, and two loads of whisky to the ferry per week. The loss of 20 distillery pay packets will be felt in the shops, pubs and service industries of Port Ellen.

Since the closure, Port Ellen Distillery has gradually been allowed to fall into disrepair. The current extent of this is plain to the eye and there is no way back for Port Ellen as a distillery. The decision to close was taken before the DCL had any inkling that there would one day be a real demand for the whisky as a single malt and its rarity is only driving up prices of bottlings as they come to the market.

A visit to what is now left of the distillery is really too depressing to undertake. You are well advised to take solace in a dram of Port Ellen in one of Islay's bars where you can consider what was and what might have been as you drain your glass. A visit to the adjoining maltings is, thankfully, a completely different prospect.

Port Ellen Distillery & Maltings

By Port Ellen, Islay, Argyll
PA42 7AJ
Tel: 01496 302 705
Fax: 01496 302 702
Owners: Diageo
Site Operations manager: John A Thomson

Visits to the Port Ellen Maltings are restricted to company, trade and press but if you feel that you have a bona fide case to see round the plant, than a phone call to John Thomson might be the key to opening the door to this fascinating operation. The tour is an all-encompassing one that takes you through the modern processes of steeping, malting and kilning in a state-of-the-art facility. The fact that the Islay distillers can request precise malting specifications and have it delivered from a local base is an enormous benefit to the distilling community.

There may be a lack of atmosphere and romance at the Maltings, but it does show how much has moved on and how standards and quality can be maintained despite large-scale production methods. The adjoining distillery is being maintained on a care and maintenance basis with any buildings dating from 1967 due to be demolished to enable the local authorities and enterprise agencies to convert the original distillery into some form of commercial premises. John Ramsay would have approved of that but I am sure he would have much preferred such a famous and historically important distillery to have been kept working doing what it did best. Port Ellen's demise remains one of the saddest in Scotland's whisky heritage.

Port Ellen Maltings

Tours of this enormous manufactory are seldom available to the public, but during the Classic Malts Cruise and the Islay Festival of Music and Malt there are opportunities to be shown round. In July 2001 I was part of the group from the CMC flotilla that was taken round by John Thomson, the site operations manager, who gave an in-depth insight into malt and the way it is made here. In his own words, this is what he told us:

One of the huge drums makes its way through Port Ellen, 1972.

In the early 1970s Scottish Malt Distillers owned three distilleries on Islay: Port Ellen, Caol Ila and Lagavulin. The company decided that the quality, quantity and cost of malt being produced by these distilleries' traditional floor maltings could be significantly improved by building a single modern maltings to supply all three distilleries' needs. Thus Port Ellen Maltings was built in 1972 and commissioned in 1973.

It was designed to supply high quality heavily peated malt to the three SMD Islay distilleries. Barley arrives at Port Ellen by boat, 750 to 1,200 tonnes at a time. Up to 650 tonnes of barley can be held temporarily in the grain silo alongside the pier. Port Ellen Maltings has nine barley silos with a combined capacity of 2,040 tonnes, approximately 2,700 tonnes including the pier silo.

To initiate malting, Port Ellen has eight steel steeps, which are cylindro-conical vessels holding 25 tonnes of barley and 30,000 litres of water each. Each steep has two aeration systems. The first system, 'suction aeration', is used to suck fresh, cool air into the steep when it contains barley but is empty of water. The second system, 'pressure aeration', is used when the barley is under water. Compressed air is blown from the bottom of the steep up through the water and barley, causing the barley to become well mixed.

To germinate the malt, Port Ellen has seven huge, steel Boby drums, each drum holding the contents of two steeps which is 50 tonnes of original barley weight or 65 tonnes of barley at 45% moisture content. These are the largest malting drums in the UK.

Large fans blow carefully controlled volumes of air through the 'green malt' in the drum at just the right temperature and humidity to provide ideal growth conditions. Every eight hours the drums take 5 minutes to do a complete rotation and so keep the malt in the drum mixed and free flowing.

To kiln the malt, Port Ellen Maltings has three kilns, each capable of holding the complete contents of a single drum. Automatically controlled burners heat the malt and peat fires provide the 'reek' (smoke) to flavour the malt. A typical, heavily peated, 50-tonne batch will require about six tonnes of peat to be burned. The peat used is harvested from Castlehill moss less than three miles across the hills from Port Ellen. The finished malt is stored in one of 31 malt silos with a combined capacity of 3,500 tonnes.

The new maltings worked normally until the early 1980s when there was a general downturn in the production of new make whisky. Many distilleries across Scotland were closed at this time and all the others went on to part-time production. At Scottish Malt Distillers, Port Ellen Distillery (closed in 1983) and Caol Ila and Lagavulin were both producing well below their maximum capacity.

At this point it appeared that the maltings might have to be closed too as it was not economic to run the plant at these low production levels. However, the other distillers on the island came to the rescue. They wished to obtain high quality Islay-produced malt from Port Ellen and so the seeds of an agreement were sown. In 1987 the Concordat of Islay Distillers was signed – a gentleman's agreement between the maltings and all the distillers on Islay and Jura, who agreed to take at least a proportion of their malt from Port Ellen Maltings – this saved the maltings from closure and gave the distilleries access to high quality Islay malt.

As part of the agreement the maltings had to produce malt to each customer's specification. Instead of producing only highly peated, direct-fired malt, the maltings now had to satisfy the requirements of eight distilleries whose specifications ranged across the entire spectrum of distilling malts from unpeated, indirect-fired, through low- and medium-peated to the more familiar highly peated and direct-fired malts. The Concordat has continued to be honoured to this day and not much has changed at Port Ellen since then.

The Port Ellen bonds, still in good nick
(upper left); the malting drums (lower left);
the old tun room (bottom left); the exterior
from the main road (above).

Bowmore

THE ESTABLISHMENT of a distillery in Bowmore at the foot of Hill Street was a natural development in the early industrial evolution of the village. With hindsight it is too easy to conclude that the modest operation, which probably started just as the village began to take shape in 1768, was of little immediate benefit to the community but after two centuries of almost continuous production the vision of the Campbells has been realised.

The early history of the distillery can only be surmised, but an understanding of the way in which many of the leases were contracted in those days leads one to believe that David Simson was distilling much earlier than 1779, as has been thought. When Daniel Campbell the 'Younger' decided to build Bowmore and move the island's social and economic centre from Killarow (now Bridgend) he granted many new leases for the village through his chief feuar, Hugh Mackay. Most of these were settled with a handshake, and remained so until the growing liabilities of tenant and laird alike made a more formal contract necessary. In Bowmore's case these written leases first appear in 1766, when Campbell had a feu charter drawn up

between himself and Simson for a 'rood of land and square acres of Moss.' These were soon supplemented with 'a piece of ground in Hill Street and Shore Street.'

In 1776, one year before he died, Daniel Campbell granted rights to Simson 'to build and erect dwelling houses and other houses and to quarry, win and load stones for these purposes, and to cut, win and load turf from the moss.'

So what happened during the 10 years between these agreements? Simson created the mould from which all the other commercially successful island distillers were drawn. He was a merchant and farmer alike and had been distilling at Killarow for some time until he quit to move to Bowmore around 1766. Donald MacEachern then took over at Killarow, and local knowledge suggests that Simson started building his new distillery almost immediately.

He clearly had a great deal of energy since he also acted as postmaster between 1767 and 1775, and claimed to be in the same position in 1790. He had also been responsible for the running of the Islay packet from Tarbert, Argyll to Port Askaig, although he was none too successful in that venture. He was far better as a distiller, and by securing a feu for Bowmore Distillery it meant that he actually owned the ground as opposed to leased it. Built during a time of common grain shortages the output of Bowmore would have reflected this influence – men like Simson did well to maintain their small operations, particularly in the face of the illicit distillers. He felt strongly about this and at the biannual meeting of the Stent Committee in March 1801, he was one of the signatories to the pledge that:

This meeting resolve collectively & individually to use their utmost exertions for preventing any of the grain of the Island being destroy'd by illegal Distillers, and for that purpose pledge themselves to inform agt any person or persons that they may know or hear to be concerned in this illegal and destructive Traffick.

Simson is believed to have extended his distilling activities to Jura for a while but this was short-lived. The distance from Bowmore and the access during the winter months created too many problems and he concentrated his business on Islay. Eventually he relinquished control to Hector Simson who had a new water course built in 1825 which the estate financed. An entry in the Rent Roll reads:

Interest to be charged to H Simson on £65, the sum expended in making Distillery Canal at 7½ per cent.

The laird further encouraged distilling by extending credit in the form of barley to Simson who repaid this when the whisky was sold in Glasgow. In 1827, barley worth £756 was advanced in this manner to Simson and rent was frequently paid to the laird by the farmers in the form of grain.

In 1837 the distillery changed hands to William and James Mutter, Glasgow merchants of German extraction, who began a programme of expansion and renovation. James Mutter was a philanthropist and a progressive farmer in the same mould as the Campbells and John Ramsay. Besides leasing three farms on Islay, he found time to be the Ottoman, Portuguese and Brazilian Vice-Consul in Glasgow.

Under the Mutters new kilns, warehouses and tun rooms were built and the stillhouse was enlarged featuring a still with forked head! The amount of water reaching the distillery was increased by rerouting the lade from the River Laggan. A local tailor is credited with overcoming the problems of a lack of fall over the new course by observing the movement of drops of water along a length of waxed thread. The resulting course of the lade is thus some nine miles (14 km) although the source is only half this distance from the distillery.

A 145-ton iron steamship, not surprisingly named the SS *James Mutter*, was commissioned to ply between Islay and Glasgow where the Mutters had warehouse facilities beneath the arches of Central Station. Bowmore became a renowned single malt sold in various export markets and in England was purveyed successfully by a number of travelling salesmen. When Barnard looked around Bowmore, the distillery was producing 200,000 gallons of spirit (908,000 litres) per annum. Only Ardbeg could boast a greater volume on the island.

The sons of the Mutter brothers ran the distillery until 1892, when it was sold to a consortium from London in a sale which was disputed. The outcome was The Bowmore Distillery Company which controlled the operation through the bleak war years until 1925 when J B Sherriff & Company bought it for £20,000. This company had originally been formed in 1895 to acquire the Lochhead Distillery in Campbeltown and the Lochindaal Distillery at Port Charlotte, along with sugar plantations and a rum distillery in Jamaica. In 1920 Sherriffs were forced into liquidation and both distilleries were acquired by Benmore Distilleries who maintained them until being absorbed by the DCL in

1929. Lochhead closed for good in 1928 followed by Lochindaal just after the DCL takeover. It was then dismantled, although the bonds still exist and are used by Caol Ila Distillery.

After the liquidation, J B Sherriff & Company Limited was sold to J P O'Brien Limited exactly one day after that firm itself had passed a resolution for voluntary liquidation. They had just purchased Bulloch, Lade, owners of Caol Ila, one month before and appear to have been in no position to hold onto assets so both J B Sherriff and Bulloch, Lade found ready buyers at knockdown prices. The name and goodwill of Sherriffs were purchased for £100 in shares by a Skye man, Duncan MacLeod of Skeabost who had also been a director of Bulloch, Lade and the Highland Bonding Company. A new company bearing the name of J B Sherriff was then formed in December 1924, purchased Bowmore the following year, and ran it under Sherriff's Bowmore Distillery Limited. The resurrection lasted until 1950 when William Grigor & Son Limited of Inverness, who had been responsible for the rebuilding of the Glen Albyn Distillery in 1884, took them over.

The intervening war years had seen the distillery unproductive, like many others, due to the government's prohibition on distilling. Bowmore was requisitioned by the Air Ministry to serve as the operations centre for Coastal Command giving anti-submarine assistance to Atlantic convoys. Bowmore was not alone amongst the island distilleries in this – Tobermory was put to use by the navy during World War I.

Stanley P Morrison Limited, the Glasgow whisky brokers, moved into distilling in 1963 by purchasing the company at a time when many disused distilleries, like Jura, were being recommissioned. The expansion of trade in the 1960s resulted in malt whisky output rising from 65 million litres of pure alcohol (LPA) to 124 million LPA in 1968. In this atmosphere Morrisons instigated a period of modernisation and expansion.

When Morrisons made their purchase, it was the first in a series of steps taking them to the forefront of the small independents in the whisky industry. The Roseburn Bonding Company was soon added to extend storage and create valuable blending facilities in Glasgow and this was followed with the Tannochside Bonding Company in 1965, where new warehousing was built to hold 5 million gallons (22.7 million litres) of spirit. Their distilling interests were further

Above: Interior of a Bowmore kiln, 1980.
Below: The distillery from the pier in 1984.

increased in 1970 when they bought Glen Garioch Distillery near Old Meldrum in Aberdeenshire from SMD, and the Auchentoshan Distillery near Glasgow, producing a triple-distilled malt which has risen to a top 10 position in the export league of bottled malts.

All island distilleries suffer from high overheads largely due to transportation costs to and from the mainland – in Bowmore's case these costs amounted to £100,000 per annum. In attempting to overcome these, Morrisons tried to find a means to offset them against savings from reduced fuel consumption. Fuel bills within the industry in 1970 accounted for some nine per cent of production costs, rising to 16 per cent by 1980. They had already had some success at Glen Garioch by employing a waste heat recovery system that was used to create perfect growing environments for tomatoes in glasshouses built next to the distillery. With a ready market for the produce in the Aberdeenshire area the project gradually expanded to 145 tonnes per annum and proved profitable while savings amounting to over £90,000 per annum were realised. (Sadly, Morrison's commitment to Glen Garioch waned as Bowmore's ascendancy continued and they were forced to close the distillery for most of 1995 only re-opening it in 1997. However, the hothouses have never been resurrected.)

With the experience gained from the Glen Garioch project, the company sought a similar solution for Bowmore. A glasshouse project was rejected due to the lack of surrounding suitable ground and the small market amongst Islay's 4,000 residents. The energy consultants Derick Sampson & Partners of Glasgow designed a waste heat recovery system which was to reduce the fuel costs by 50 per cent with a payback on capital investment in less than three years.

The new system operated on the principle that steam could be created at low temperatures in the presence of a vacuum located in the vapour head on the still condensers. Sufficient quantities of 'flash' steam were thus generated not only to heat the stills, but also the coppers. Another benefit was the conversion of the kiln to indirect heating by means of a water/air heat exchanger drawing hot water from the condensers surplus to process requirements, eliminating completely the heavy fuel oil which was then in use as the primary heat source.

The capital outlay required was £274,000 but annual fuel savings were estimated to run to £104,500. These were very attractive figures for Morrisons' board to contemplate but there was one major drawback – the effect that the change in the way the stills were heated would have on the whisky. Despite this reservation the plan was approved in early 1983, with installation taking place during the annual shutdown in the summer.

Did this affect the character of Bowmore? Some might say it did, but then the range of expressions of Bowmore has expanded to such a degree since my visit in the 80s, that it is well-nigh impossible to determine exactly what effect it might have had. In 1984 only a single UK home trade bottling was available on the market along with a number of rare vintage expressions. One of them, a 1956 from a sherry cask was given to me by Jim McEwan in the distillery office when I revisited Islay to complete research on *Scotch and Water*. I will never forget that dram. It was simply sensational and remains imprinted in my tastebud memory banks to this day.

Since the mid-1980s the distillery has evolved gradually. A community swimming pool has been built in a bonded warehouse that was donated by Morrisons for the purpose. Waste heat from the distilling process warms the water and it has become a major educational and leisure facility for Islay and Jura. Since my visit Bowmore has surged into the top-selling range of malts worldwide. One of the major reasons for this success was Jim McEwan.

Trained as a cooper from 1963 at Bowmore, Jim became warehouse manager in 1969 and ran the cellars until 1977 when he moved to Glasgow to spend the next seven years as a blender. He returned to Islay as distillery manager in 1984 and began to take the distillery to a higher level as the company broadened its export base.

The view up to Bowmore's round church from the pier.

Jim McEwan is the epitome of the archetypal Islay distiller. He has a passion for malt whisky that is legendary and his later role at Bowmore was to take that passion around the world and win the hearts and minds of whisky drinkers everywhere. To see Jim at work at one of his masterclasses is to witness a real expert. By the end of the evening even the most sceptical critic is won over. I once attended such an event at Bowmore in the company of an East-coast American dentist who had been shocked on flying over Islay to see such clear, turquoise waters below. 'I'm not looking forward to this though … an hour and a half of talking whisky … ugh!' 'Just you wait mate,' I thought and sure enough, an hour and a half later he skipped up to me and said, 'That was the most entertaining evening I've had in years!' But don't take my word for it…go and see Jim at a whisky event for yourself.

Bowmore Distillery

School Street
Bowmore, Islay, Argyll
PA43 7JS
Tel: 01496 810441
Fax: 01496 810757
www.morrisonbowmore.co.uk
Owners: Morrison Bowmore Distillers Ltd
Manager: Ian McPherson

SUCH a central location on Islay means that Bowmore is the island's busiest stop for whisky enthusiasts. It has everything going for it and the quality of the tour is second to none. Personality abounds here. Anyone who has visited the distillery in the past decade will have met Christine Logan, an Ileach who is better known in Japan than in Scotland. Christine is the public face of Bowmore and once met, she is never forgotten.

Her dedication and commitment led to her being the guest of the Japanese Bartenders' Guild in late 2002 when she spent 10 days touring the country visiting Suntory plants, talking to the press and generally, 'being treated like royalty' as Christine told me. 'It was the trip of a lifetime, one that told me so much about the Japanese people and their culture. One wee whisky bar that I visited could only hold six people maximum, but the owner held several times the required stock turnover of every malt imaginable. How on earth could he justify that in commercial terms? Their passion for the product is immense … they are light years ahead of us over here.'

Maybe so, but Bowmore was one of the first distilleries to employ new production techniques in order to push the efficiencies further and take it up to the highest quality levels of single malt whisky production and yet still have that essential mix of the old and the new.

This existence of new techniques within the framework of such an old distillery makes it one of the most rewarding of all to visit. The bonds, however, remain unchanged, no modern influences can alter the way in which whisky matures. To the rear of the stillhouse, through a cramped alley, the old vaults lie, sunk deep into the sloping ground. Inside, row upon row of butts and hogsheads are racked in the traditional matter by 'dunnage'. The Queen has had whisky bonded here for her in the past and Islay malt is no stranger to the Royal Household – on Christmas Eve 1841 this letter was sent from Windsor Castle to the laird:

My Dear Islay,
Will you undertake a commission and oblige me by ordering or procuring for me (or rather for the Queen's Cellar) a cask of your best Islay Mountain Dew? I am not very particular as to the exact quantity contained by the cask nor as to the price, but I want the very best that can be had, for which reason I prefer troubling you to ordering it blindfold from any merchant ... We are all in great turmoil here preparing for the reception of all sorts of Royalties and Principalities at the Christening of the P of Wales. I expect no peace or quiet till it is over!
Believe me my dear chief
Yrs very faithfully
Ch A Murray

The 'Dew' was obviously a great favourite at the palace – just over two years later Murray repeated the request for another 120 gallons (545 litres), beseeching Campbell to put the distiller 'on his mettle to give us his best brew ... ' and reminding him to pay particular attention to the 'Excise Drawback, for the Queen's spirits pay no duty ... '! It was in fact John Ramsay who supplied the palace with a special 21-year-old vatted malt which he called 'Dunaid'. He named this extraordinary whisky after Dunaid, a small promontory on the southern side of the Oa that he considered to be Islay's most interesting antiquity. The Oa abounds with names of Norse origin and Ramsay felt that Dunaid was the most likely site of any island court which the Norsemen might have held since it so

Hand-turning the malt with a shiel.

closely resembled Thingvalla in Iceland which was used for that purpose. The small neck of land joining Dunaid to the mainland would have been easily defended by a small number of armed men, making a surprise attack impossible. Later, the Lords of the Isles employed the same strategy at Finlaggan by holding court on the islet in the Loch.

The whisky itself was an interesting marriage of Port Ellen (which could only have been 16 years old at the most) and 21-year-old Upper Cragabus, which Ramsay claimed was the finest whisky every produced on Islay. Unfortunately a great deal of the production from this area was illicit and there is a good chance that some of this may have found its way into the Royal cask. When the MacCuaigs were producing legal whisky at Cragabus (see Appendix 3 on page 134) it is reputed that the profits from the exports to Ireland went into establishing the White Hart Hotel in Port Ellen.

Bowmore remains one of my favourite drams and it is now available in a plethora of expressions, many of them backed with high-profile advertising campaigns that evoke the folklore of Islay. Too many to enjoy at one sitting? With that sobering thought in mind, a visit to the Lochside Hotel in Shore Street to sample some of them from the huge selection behind the bar confirms that this need never be the case.

Bruichladdich, Bunnahabhain and Caol Ila

ALL THREE distilleries share their names with small villages that were built up around them, creating their own communities dependent on them for employment. In the case of Caol Ila and Bunnahabhain in particular, it is likely that without the distilleries there would have been no sustained human interference in the area at all. There, the workers' houses were constructed at the same time as the distilleries, and even today are almost all owned by the companies operating the plants.

Caol Ila lies just north of Port Askaig on the Sound of Islay at the end of a tortuous cul-de-sac overlooking the Paps of Jura. It was built in 1846 by a Glasgow businessman with extensive distilling interests. Hector Henderson had been a partner in the Campbeltown Distillery in 1837, and having just withdrawn from the Littlemill Distillery near Bowling, Dunbartonshire, was looking for a suitable site for a new distillery and, for reasons known only to himself, he chose the remote Islay location. It is a surprising site for a distillery and

when Alfred Barnard made his way to Caol Ila in 1886 the approach had not changed in 40 years:

We soon came in sight of the distillery lying directly beneath us, and we wonder for a moment how we are to get down to it. Our driver, however, knew the road well, for often had he been here before, and turning sharp to the right, we commenced the descent through the little hamlet of houses. But the way is so steep and our nerves none of the best, that we insist upon doing the remainder of the descent on foot, much to the disgust of the driver, who muttered strange words in Gaelic. His remarks, however, are lost upon us, that language not having formed part of our education. As we descended the hill, we paused now and then to gaze upon the far stretching view before us, and to rest. Presently we found ourselves at the object of our search, and within a few yards of the sea. Caol Ila Distillery stands in the wildest and most picturesque locality we have seen. It is situated on the Sound of

Islay on the very verge of the sea, in a deep recess of the mountain mostly cut out of the solid rock. The coast hereabouts is wild and broken, and detached pieces of rock lie here and there of such size that they form small islands.

To the Victorian reader this description was very much in the style of the times, but to be fair to Barnard the route is largely unchanged today, and is still impressive.

Henderson may have been attracted by the exceptionally pure source of water from Torrabolls Loch, but it is more likely that the laird, his estate on the verge of bankruptcy, recognised a perfectly good opportunity to extend Islay's distilling industry which had become a major source of employment on the island. After the worst depression of the 19th century, during which 61 distilleries closed between 1835 and 1844, confidence in the malt sector in the face of increasing competition from the Lowland distillers was very low. However, the Islay malts were still highly regarded as flavoursome drams in comparison to the bland Lowland whisky. Walter Frederick Campbell, for his part, had helped establish or legalise around a dozen distilleries during his lairdship of Islay though not all of them had lasted as long as he would have liked. These included Daill, Newton, Tallant, Lossit and Mulindry which were all large farm distilleries with illicit beginnings.

In 1847 Henderson sunk his money not only into Caol Ila but also Camlachie Distillery, Glasgow, and installed larger pot stills two years later. In 1849 the

The crew of the JDL, July 2001.

ground lease for Caol Ila was granted to an unknown William Campbell, who may possibly have been a financier in the same style as many of the Kildalton operators, and by 1850 Henderson had entered a partnership to acquire Lochindaal Distillery at Port Charlotte. All the signs point to Henderson extending his business too quickly, and by 1852 Henderson

Opening day, 29th May, 2001.

Bruichladdich Distillery

Bruichladdich, Islay, Argyll
PA49 7UN
Tel: 01496 850221
Fax: 01496 850477
www.bruichladdich.com
Owners: Murray McDavid
Manager: Duncan McGillivray

AT BRIDGEND the road to the 'other side' of Islay branches off and skirts the raised beaches around the head of the loch. Sheltered in mature woodland and straddling the River Sorn at a natural ford, the tiny village consists of a grocery, garden store, hotel, bowling green and a few houses on the bank of the river, but until 1768 it was the centre of Islay's commerce. The likely site of David Simson's Killarow Distillery is the house next to the bridge, and the long barn across the road next to the hotel was probably used as the maltings.

Lamont and Company was forced to stop trading altogether.

The industry at this time was having to contend with an influential temperance movement with widespread support and a government which sought to equalise the duty on spirits throughout the United Kingdom. This meant that Scottish producers had to withstand rises in duty which brought them up to the higher levels at which the English had operated for many years. Some distillers could not absorb these increases and, coupled with a general decline in whisky consumption in

A couple of miles down the A847 from Bridgend, the low whitewashed façade of Bruichladdich Distillery comes into view. Entry is through an attractive wrought iron gate, opening to reveal a spacious and almost totally enclosed courtyard. The distillery offices are on an upper floor above the filling store overlooking the seafront. The floor maltings run the length of the greater part of the front of the distillery, and it is here that Jim McEwan's malt whisky academy is being established. To the left-hand side of the courtyard, the main processes are carried out. By entering the mash-house to the rear and proceeding along the length of the building, a good understanding of them can be obtained. The beautiful wooden washbacks lie in the next room, followed by the equally attractive stillhouse containing the four stills set square into the raised pine floor and complemented by the wood-beamed roof. Two spirit safes sitting between the pairs of stills afford the stillman an economy of effort. The company 'colours' of the new Bruichladdich are everywhere (even the roller mill has had the treatment) and reflect the azure waters of Loch Indaal. Jim's plan is to create more expressions of Bruichladdich, some of which will reflect the heavier peated style that was once made, and stocks are being laid down to ensure supplies

Now available at 10, 15, 17 and 20 years, along with limited expressions from 1984, 1970 and 1966, Bruichladdich is greatly sought after. Traditionally one of the lighter Islays, the previous owner's 15-year-old

Scotland, they folded. Between 1850 and 1857, there were over 30 closures in Scotland, most of which occurred in rural areas where they had used locally-grown barley, thus benefiting from the malt drawback until Gladstone abolished it in 1855.

Collapses of this nature had a restricting effect on the industry in general, but the sequestration of Henderson Lamont & Company did at least allow Norman Buchanan of the Jura Distillery to take over Caol Ila. Buchanan was barely set up in Jura when Henderson went under, so he jumped at the chance to enter an almost new plant just across the Sound. When his business was sequestrated in 1863 he was probably wishing he had concentrated on Jura – once more Caol Ila was ownerless.

In the meantime developments had taken place at Henderson's other distillery at Camlachie. It had been purchased by Bulloch and Company, who were trading three years later as Bulloch, Lade and Company and were to remain in control for the next 61 years. When Caol Ila came on the market in 1863 they acquired it, realising an excellent opportunity to buy a malt which

Bruichladdich's relative youth of 120 years explains its more favoured position on Loch Indaal's western shore.

bottling remains one of my favourites, but is is a fast-disappearing dram, so get hold of a bottle now!

Bruichladdich pier lies a short walk from the distillery. Although it used to serve both Bruichladdich and Lochindaal distilleries, the most frequent visitor from the mainland is now the oil tanker offloading the island's supply into the nearby storage tanks. Down at Port Charlotte, a relic from the days of illicit distilling lies in the far corner of the Museum of Islay Life – a small pot still complete with its worm. When it was presented to the Museum's librarian Gordon Booth, the hills behind McArthur's Head were pointed out and he was quietly informed that the still ' … came from up there.'

Behind the village at Octomore, George Montgomery was distilling during the early part of the 19th century. This distillery was one of the many established during Walter Frederick Campbell's lairdship after the Small Stills Act of 1816, but it eventually closed after Thomas Pattison quit in 1852. That left the distillery in Port Charlotte, having the better shore-side location, as the only one active in the immediate vicinity. The distillery was exactly 100 years

old when it was closed by the DCL in 1929 and dismantled. Only the warehouses at the northern end of the village give any indication of that century of activity.

Returning to Bridgend, the A846 is rejoined and leads not only to Bunnahabhain and Caol Ila, but also to the sites of a couple of the other distilleries active in the early 19th century. As the road rises out of the woods at Bridgend a farm track appears on the right just after the junction on the left for Eallabus (the Islay Estate farm). At the end of the track one finds a well-proportioned house but the rearmost outbuilding has a roof reminiscent of a pagoda-topped kiln. Could it have once been a kiln? Possibly, since this is Newton where Neil MacEachern distilled, apparently without a convenient water source – small wonder he didn't stay long. Further up the A846, a right turn at Ballygrant leads behind Loch Ballygrant to Lossit Kennels which used to be the site of Lossit Distillery. Records show that on 30th October 1833, Malcolm McNeill despatched 10 and a quarter gallons of Lossit aqua to William Cunningham for the sum of £5 2s 6d, or 10 shillings a gallon. (See Appendix 2 on page 130.)

Bruichladdich in 1984.

had a good reputation in the growing blending trade. Bulloch, Lade were even then a large company dealing mainly with the trade as blenders and commission agents, with outlets at home and abroad. Their success enabled them to build the Benmore Distillery in Campbeltown in 1868 and carry out major improvements at Caol Ila in 1879. At the time of Barnard's visit, it was one of the most modern in existence, producing 147,000 gallons (667,000 litres) per annum.

The 1880s represented a decade of expansion for the malt producers. Blended whiskies were then so well accepted that they sold in almost every country in the world – some of them with brand names still in existence today. Many of the heavy island malts were used by blenders to mask the bland Lowland whiskies in their products and thus give them more character. This growing demand for malt led to the distillers expanding out of their low capital investment operations and building units capable of higher outputs. Other Lowland distillers like Bulloch, Lade looked for suitable opportunities to expand their business. This led

to the construction of both Bruichladdich and Bunnahabhain.

Bruichladdich was built in 1881 by Robert, William and John Gourlay Harvey with money from a trust fund set up by their father, William Harvey Jnr. The family had been in the distilling business for some time in the Yoker and Dundashill distilleries in Glasgow. The construction of the distillery and the improvements made at Caol Ila two years before were unique in that a newly-patented building material, modern concrete, was being put to one of its first uses on the island.

Bunnahabhain was designed from the start as a high output malt distillery with a product principally aimed at the blenders in Glasgow and until a change of ownership in 1961, it distilled a typical heavily-peated spirit. Formed as the Islay Distillery Company in 1881, and incorporated the next year, the partners of this firm spent a great deal of money establishing Bunnahabhain as a premier malt. An entire village grew up around the distillery, complete with schoolhouse and village hall. A link road to the main Bridgend – Port Askaig road was put down as well as a 'commodious and handsome pier at a cost of about £3,500' which was greatly admired by Alfred Barnard. He was also less apprehensive about the approach to Bunnahabhain compared to Caol Ila and clearly felt that the distillery represented the very best in progressive Victorian industrialisation, '… this portion of the island was bare, and uninhabited, but the prosecution of the distilling industry has transformed it into a life-like and civilised colony.' In fact, not long after Bunnahabhain was established another proposal was put to the Islay Estate for the building of a distillery due north of Bunnahabhain at Rubha Bhaclaig but this came to nought.

The enclosed square format of Bunnahabhain's design was reflected in the distillery at Bruichladdich which Barnard entered 'through an archway' into a central courtyard. Not much has changed since – any alterations have been largely within the plant and the external appearance remains the same, although the centrally situated kiln no longer exists and the floor maltings are now silent.

Within a short period, the business of all three distilleries was consolidated. Bulloch, Lade had not only successfully promoted Caol Ila as single bottled malt to compete with the likes of Smith's Glenlivet and Mutter's Bowmore, but had also pushed their BL blend to the top. With the encouragement of W A Robertson of Robertson & Baxter, the partnership operating Bunnahabhain amalgamated in 1887 with W Grant of the Glenrothes-Glenlivet Distillery to form the Highland Distilleries Limited, and thus increase the group's malt whisky output to 400,000 gallons (1,800,000 litres) per annum. Robertson supported the move by becoming a leading customer. By 1886 the Harvey family had formed the Bruichladdich Distillery Company (Islay Limited) with a share capital of £24,000 spread amongst five Harveys who then controlled Bruichladdich, Yoker and Dundashill Distilleries. The last of these had, for many years, remained the largest pot-still distillery in the Lowlands. Bulloch, Lade's output from Camlachie (by then renamed Loch Katrine) and Caol Ila was in excess of 440,000 gallons (2,000,000 litres) of spirit per year. Throughout the late 1880s, the malt whisky trade enjoyed increased production but this was to change

dramatically at the end of the century.

With the increasing consumption of blended whiskies, an aggressive new dimension in marketing took shape. Blenders like Buchanans, Charles Mackinlay and Company, John Walker & Sons Limited, and Dewars of Perth sold brands abroad with some cunning and great success. Names like the 'Pinch', and Mackie's 'White Horse' were familiar sights at home and overseas. But success adversely affected Bulloch, Lade for a while when demand for their BL brand ran down stocks to the point where the whisky was unavailable.

Blenders started exchanging fillings to satiate the market and new distilleries began to spring up, almost all of them in Speyside. The problems of locality, transport, construction costs and distance from the city markets were overriding factors to any blender looking for a suitable site for a new distillery. The modern railway system serving the Highlands made for easy communication with the Lowlands and England and most important of all, the public were beginning to demand a lighter blended whisky, and that meant going to Speyside for malt.

The boom years finally came to an end with the close of the century and the collapse of the Pattisons of Leith in December 1898. Many investors and speculators

Bunnahabhain in 1984.

were left broke in the wake of the scandal which destroyed confidence in the trade in general. The DCL, formed in 1877 as an amalgamation of giant Lowland distilling interests, strengthened their resolve to safeguard the industry against a repetition of this nature, and embarked upon a programme of rationalisation which formed the basis of the modern industry as it exists today. With distilleries up for sale, and sequestrations commonplace, the DCL moved in, bought up, and closed many of them in an effort to control the industry's output. To this end, the Harveys were approached by the DCL in 1901, during the Depression following the Boer War, to sell their Dundashill Distillery that had just been converted to a patent-still operation. They rejected the move and closed the plant, but just two years later found themselves firmly in the DCL fold while still retaining control of Bruichladdich. Their interest in the Yoker Distillery had diminished, until it was closed in 1906, leaving them solely with their Islay base.

Meanwhile, a unique relationship had developed between Highland Distilleries and Robertson & Baxter Limited whereby the distiller's marketing was handled by the Glasgow blenders, while they remained independent of each other. Altogether the number of productive distilleries in Scotland dropped from 161 in 1899 to 132 by 1908 whilst the DCL continued to trim the industry – a measure which probably saw it through World War I. Although the industry responded selflessly to the war effort by switching to the production of industrial alcohol, its contribution was never fully appreciated by a man who, ideally, would have preferred to have seen distilling prohibited – Lloyd George.

Prohibition did occur in 1917, some firms never fully recovering, but the facts of life were explained in a very straight manner to Lloyd George by William Ross of the DCL, and he ditched the more extreme of his proposals for control of alcohol production. Nevertheless, Bulloch, Lade & Company went into voluntary liquidation in 1920, with £½ million stock in trade selling out to J P O'Brien Limited who, on the point of liquidation themselves, immediately turned the company over to a consortium headed by the DCL, Dewars, Watsons of Dundee, W P Lowrie, managed by Robertson & Baxter, and known as the Caol Ila Distillery Company Limited. The other Bulloch, Lade distilleries at Loch Katrine and Benmore were sold off, the former to the DCL and the latter to the owners of Lochindaal Distillery, Benmore Distilleries, who kept it open until 1927.

By 1929, the effects of prohibition in the United States forced Robertson & Baxter to sell off their entire stocks to Buchanan-Dewar, the DCL and John Walker & Sons, and with the stock went Haig & Haig's revered 'Pinch' brand. Their shares in Caol Ila were taken up by Dewars, John Walker & Sons (who had just entered the consortium), and W P Lowrie. The shares of Watsons of Dundee, who had also just gone into liquidation were disposed of similarly. Any firms within the industry with cash flow problems were realising their assets at this time and invariably it was the DCL and its associates that snapped them up.

This setback did not deter Robertson & Baxter from exploiting the market in the United States through whatever loopholes could be found. Using lines of supply created by the bootleggers, whisky was smuggled into the country from Canada and the Bahamas. One of Robertson & Baxter's London customers, Berry Bros, managed to find one such line of supply which was to prove invaluable to themselves and their suppliers after the repeal of prohibition in 1933. 'Cutty Sark' was first blended by Robertson & Baxter for Berry Bros in 1923, who actually owned the label. It was a successful brand from the start, in great demand in the States during prohibition,

Bunnahabhain Distillery

Port Askaig, Islay, Argyll
PA46 7RP
Tel: 01496 840646
Fax: 01496 840248
Owners: Burn Stewart Distillers Ltd
Manager: John MacLellan

THE TURN-OFF for Bunnahabhain from the A846 is just a little before the Caol Ila junction as you go from Kiells to Port Askaig. The road down to the distillery is more treacherous than the Caol Ila approach in that it is entirely single-tracked with a number of blind bends. To admire the view up the Sound to Colonsay, it is best to park and not risk meeting a supply lorry trying to catch a ferry for Kennacraig. The road winds past Persabus Farm, Loch nam Ban (Torrabolls Loch, the Caol Ila water supply) and over the top of the cliffs near Rubha a'Mhill, beneath which the rusting hulk of the Wyre Majestic lies grounded and rotting since 1974. Far up the Sound, the Rhuval lighthouse, built in 1859, gives better warning to those rounding Islay's most northerly point, Rubha a'Mhail.

When I visited Bunnahabhain in April 1984 the SS *Monica*, under a Honduran flag, could be seen unloading malt from Eire, the first for two years, a sight reminiscent of the earliest days of production at Bunnahabhain over a century before. Then the pier was busy with ships bringing barley from the most unlikely locations. The boom on which Bunnahabhain was built also created shortages in home-grown barley, so a great deal had to be imported. The first ever mash used here was only partly Scottish barley, the remainder coming from Poland, Denmark and Russia.

The enclosed courtyard gives a claustrophobic air to the distillery, but this is more than likely due to the need to conserve ground. Outside the plant, the aspect is much more pleasant, with the ever-present Paps commanding the horizon, and the broad gentle sweep of the bay creating a welcome contrast to the rugged coastline on either side. Bunnahabhain is the end of the road for the car traveller in this part of Islay, but beyond lies a region of remote beauty open to anybody willing to pack their belongings in a rucksack for a day.

The feeling that Bunnahabhain has been left out of the bigger corporate strategy is hard to deny as the machinations of the owners over the past few years has meant that the brand-building for Black Bottle has been a stop-start process. After investing heavily in altering the product and advertising it nationally, everything seemed to go on the back burner. Rumours of its sale were spreading through the trade in late 2002 and as we were going to press I received information that a sale had been concluded.

Despite introducing limited bottlings of 1965, 1966 and 1968 which have proved successful and have raised the profile of the distillery amongst connoisseurs, it seemed ironic that at the same time as the sale, John MacLellan received the *Scottish Field* Merchants' Challenge Award for the 1968 expression which beat its famous Edrington group stablemates Macallan and Highland Park. Perhaps this wonderful malt, my favourite pre-prandial dram, is due a new lease of life. It deserves it.

The Pibroch at Caol Ila.

closed immediately, and did not re-open until 1937.

Bruichladdich finally succumbed to the effects of the Depression and locked its stills in 1929. However, prohibition in the States had caused Joseph Hobbs to look towards Scotland with a view to supplying the needs of a huge potential market after the repeal, which many people in the industry regarded as inevitable. Hobbs had had mixed fortunes during prohibition, for although he returned to his native Scotland in 1931 having lost money in the Depression (despite being the DCL's Canadian agent for a while), his ship, the *Littlehorn,* had managed to run over 130,000 cases of Teachers whisky from Antwerp to San Francisco. With his intimate knowledge of the needs of the American whisky drinker, he gained the backing of the National Distillers of America to buy up distilleries through their blenders and merchants, Train & MacIntyre. With his partners Hatim Attari and Alexander Tolmie he bought out the Harveys for £23,000 in 1937 and transferred management to Train & MacIntyre's subsidiary, Associated Scottish Distillers. His final tally included Glenury Royal Distillery (1936), Glenlochy (1937), North Esk in Montrose (1938), with Train & MacIntyre adding Fettercairn, Benromach and Strathdee in the same year.

Caol Ila was closed again in 1941, followed by Bruichladdich and Bunnahabhain shortly afterwards as a result of wartime restrictions on the amount of grain made available for distilling. Only 44 distilleries were operating in 1942, with most of the produce being shipped across the Atlantic as a valuable dollar earner for the government, which continued to raise the duty on spirits for the home market. By 1944, the situation had begun to improve a little, but exports were still the priority, and as soon as distilleries could be recommissioned, they were. Rationing of whisky for the home market forced blenders and distillers to sell the whisky abroad. Malt output rose to over 3.6 million proof gallons (13.3 million litres) in 1944, increasing to almost 6 million gallons (27.2 million litres) the following year when Caol Ila, Bunnahabhain and Bruichladdich were all active again.

when any amount of unpalatable hootch was being knocked up in back yards and barns.

Wishing to protect the reputation of their brand, (and no doubt ensure that the discerning American whisky drinker would know exactly what to ask for when prohibition ended) Francis Berry managed to secure the services of one Captain Bill McCoy who was running contraband into the States from Nassau. McCoy had a reputation for dealing only in the genuine article and under his pilotage 'Cutty Sark' remained 'the real McCoy' for thousands of thirsty Americans.

After the amalgamation of Buchanan-Dewar and John Walker with the DCL in 1925 it was inevitable that control of Caol Ila would eventually pass to the parent company. In 1927, the DCL took over after extensive improvements had been made. Management was then passed to the wholly-owned DCL subsidiary, Scottish Malt Distillers, who gained the entire shareholding, worth some £40,000, in 1930. It was then

A magnificent view of Caol Ila in the late 1960s.

Bruichladdich saw another change in ownership in 1952, when Associated Scottish Distillers sold the distillery to the Glasgow whisky brokers Ross & Coulter and thus, by chance, once more avoiding the DCL's control (they acquired Train & MacIntyre in 1953). The increased investment apparent in the 1960s and 70s brought new owners to the distillery: in 1960 A B Grant's Bruichladdich Proprietors Limited (who dropped the peaty style and closed the maltings in 1961), followed by the Invergordon Distillers in 1969. Bunnahabhain's output was doubled in 1963 with another pair of massive stills and Caol Ila was subjected to a huge reconstruction programme in the early 1970s when SMD demolished the main buildings, bar the magnificent warehouse and in their place erected a 'new distillery which would retain the architectural character of its predecessor…' That the new structure was bold, there can be no doubt, but the old pagoda

roofs and floor maltings which had been such fitting landmarks on the Sound of Islay are sadly missed by many. Barnard would feel uncomfortable with the modern block of industrial buildings dwarfed by a boiler chimney as they stand today.

By 1975, Invergordon Distillers had enlarged the mash-house and tun room at Bruichladdich without altering the original roofline, which they shared with the stillhouse, to which a new pair of stills was added. With this new plant installed, Bruichladdich's potential output approached 800,000 gallons (3.6 million litres) of proof spirit contributing to the formidable total of 5 million gallons (22.7 million litres) which, given the conditions, Islay was capable of producing each year. These conditions were rarely present during the 1980s and early 1990s, demonstrating the problem of predicting accurately the market demand years in advance and adjusting to meet it. The casual visitor to

Caol Ila, Bunnahabhain and Bruichladdich could not fail to notice that they were not working at full throttle.

The effects of this over-capacity finally manifested themselves on the Sound of Islay in March 1982 when Highland Distilleries closed Bunnahabhain, with the loss of 15 jobs. Six men were kept on to carry out warehousing and maintenance but the atmosphere over the village was soured. Workers were reputedly asked not to talk to the press – a situation for which Highland Distilleries later apologised. The redundant workers stayed on in the company-owned houses with free rent and fuel, the inference being that should production start again, they would be re-employed ' … but we can't enter into any commitments … ', a company spokesman said at the time.

The malt sector had shrunk from 83.7% of its potential output in 1978 to 38.6% in 1982 and Bunnahabhain alone could have contributed around 4% of this total working at full capacity, but there were 116 other malt distilleries in the same position and closures became a hard, common fact of life. Caol Ila was more fortunate and avoided the DCL closures of early 1983, but lost three men out of a workforce of 23 when, like Lagavulin, it switched to a four-day week.

Bruichladdich escaped closure until after the 1983 annual shutdown, but had already been working a five-day week for two years as many other independent companies had taken remedial action in advance of the drastic surgery carried out by the DCL. Many industry analysts felt at the time that the closures signified that the worst was over, and the end of a gradual 'period of retrenchment' was in sight. For the workers at Bunnahabhain, the worst was not over until the first week of April 1984 when production was reinstated on a week on/week off basis. This tentative beginning was a reaction to

Caol Ila Distillery

Port Askaig, Islay, Argyll
PA46 7RL
el: 01496 840207
Fax: 01496 840660
www.malts.com
Owners: Diageo
Manager: Billy Stitchell

Caol Ila can only be approached from the A846, where it is clearly signposted just over the back of the hill from Port Askaig. The switchback road descends behind the distillery and runs along the front of the Victorian warehouse, the only remnant of the original block before the rebuilding of the 1970s. In terms of efficiency the programme was a success, with the very latest plant installed and seawater heat exchangers employed to cool the water from the condensers. In all, over £1 million was spent with four new stills added to the original pair in a glass-fronted stillhouse looking out over the Sound to Jura.

In 1984 Grant Carmichael was on hand to show me round the plant. Nowadays, you might be lucky enough to have Billy Stitchell take you round. Diageo are slowly addressing the facilities at Caol Ila for visitors but these are unlikely to have the Skakel & Skakel treatment as Caol Ila is not one of the Classic Malts.

However, this lack of hardcore facilities give you a better impression of a working distillery and a tour of the main building quickly familiarises the visitor with all the articles used in a modern distillery of this type. Oregon pine washbacks stand adjacent to the mashtun, both under the supervision of the mashman and brewer, who maintains complete control over the operation from a central console situated on the topmost floor of the mashroom. The massive washbacks are impressive, especially to peer into when empty, but this immaculate room cannot bear comparison to the stillhouse, which is best entered on the uppermost level from the mashroom. A line of six huge gleaming copper stills meets you, their lyne arms stretching back towards the rear of the room creating a dramatic contrast with the scenery viewed through the front of the stillhouse. Despite the intimidating size of the stills, control is again completely centralised from a panel set just behind the middle pair of stills. There can be few shop floors in Scotland quite like this one.

The offices are set apart from the stillhouse with Billy poised literally over the sea wall. The 'bay' window aptly describes the view from here. Caol Ila is built in the next cove to Freeport, where in 1772, Pennant found the miner Freebairn, who had been smelting lead there since 1763. The waterfall behind the distillery which supplies Caol Ila comes from the same source which Freebairn used. These historical associations are hard to imagine against the blatantly modern design of Caol Ila, but despite this it remains one of the most rewarding to visit, not least for its location.

Jura lies across the Sound, a short ferry ride away from Port Askaig. This was the major droving halt well into the 19th century for all the cattle leaving Islay. John MacCulloch aptly described the mayhem that met him when he took the ferry to Feolin in 1824:

The shore was covered with cattle; and while some were collected in groups under the trees and rocks, crowding to avoid the hot rays of a July evening, others

were wading in the sea to shun the flies, some embarking, and another set swimming on shore from the ferry-boats; while the noise of the drovers and the boatmen, and all the bustle and vociferation which whisky did not tend to diminish, were re-echoed from hill to hill, contrasting strangely with the silence and solitude of the surrounding mountains. The disembarkation formed a most extraordinary spectacle. I had seated myself with my back to the horned company, meditating thoughts oblivious of bulls and boats alike, when I was startled by a plunge under my nose, on which uprose from bottom of the deep a cow, and with such a bound as almost to clear the entire surface. For an instant I forgot myself, and thought it was the very Water Bull of which I had heard. The very long minute that intervened between the plunge of each and its reappearance above the water, as they were all thrown over in succession, was almost awful; and their extreme buoyancy was indicated by the elastic and forcible spring with which they rose above the surface, to fall back again into the sea.

And this was six years after the Stent Committee limited the amount of whisky allowed to the ferrymen to a single mutchkin, or three-quarters of a Scots pint for every 30 head of cattle ferried! Before 1818, their allowance was unlimited, and the Stent Committee eventually decided that this was ' ... often injurious to the cattle and the proprietors thereof'. What about the ferrymen?

Caol Ila stills being loaded in Glasgow, 1974.

signs of a modest increase in malt whisky consumption at home and abroad. In January 1984 exports of bottled malt whisky increased by 86.5% to 289,000 litres per annum. The DCL made no move to increase production at Caol Ila but the smaller companies were better placed to react and Bruichladdich started producing again in early 1984, continuing until the second week of April when it closed for the annual shutdown.

At the end of that year whisky exports were up by a modest 1% overall, but the malts had advanced by a dramatic 25% overseas. The Italians confirmed their growing taste for malt whisky, buying 51% more than the previous year, making them the largest consumers in the world. Spectacular increases of more than 100% took place in Mexico, Iraq, Brazil and Paraguay, confirming the growing awareness of malt whisky abroad.

It seemed unlikely when I visited in 1984 that these distilleries would ever make use of their full production capacity again, but visiting them did at least instil a feeling of some confidence in the observer. Almost 100 years after Alfred Barnard had made the same journey, one felt that having survived the very worst, they were in a better position than most to grapple with the global economics of the 1990s.

Caol Ila, Bunnahabhain and Bruichladdich all made it through to the millennium, but they had hardly been at full throttle during the last decade. Caol Ila has remained in the Diageo portfolio and Bunnahabhain has been kept under Highland Distilleries/Edrington Group ownership. But it is Bruichladdich that has re-emerged from the brink to become a productive Islay distillery again. The story is well worth the telling. Bruichladdich became part of Jim Beam Brands (Greater Europe plc) in 1997 after the takeover of Whyte & Mackay by its parent company American Brands in 1990. The marriage was never a happy one and divorce proceedings commenced when it became apparent that the American owners did not really understand the Whyte and Mackay heritage and brand strengths. The word got round that Bruichladdich was up for grabs and an enterprising group of young (and not so young!) wine trade merchants and Scotch enthusiasts decided to table a bid. The asking price was £4.3m.

Mark Reynier of the independent bottlers Murray McDavid was one of the driving forces behind the plan and commenced discussions with Brian Megson of JBB in January 2000. This was to be Mark's second tilt at a distillery, having tried to acquire Ardbeg when Allied Distillers were trying to sell it in 1997. Mark's first job was to convince the Bank of Scotland that he was serious and they offered a letter of support on the basis that he would raise substantial funds from other investors. However, Mark got the distinct impression that the bank did not seriously expect him to succeed in raising the funding.

Along with his business colleague Simon Coughlin he began making the rounds of potential investors and also persuaded Jim McEwan to leave Morrison Bowmore Distillers and join the new company should they raise the required capital. Gradually the package came together with 50% of the equity being sourced in Scotland and one-third of that coming from residents on Islay. On December 19th, 2000 Mark waited in the JBB offices in Glasgow for confirmation that the funding was in place. The midday deadline approached and calls to his bankers had drawn a blank as expected funds had failed to materialise. It looked as though it

was all going pear-shaped when a final desperate call confirmed that the last piece of the financial jigsaw had fallen into place. The tension broken, Brian Megson then witnessed the strange spectacle of Mark screaming, jumping and leaping around his executive offices in Dalmore House as the news sunk in. He had just bought Bruichladdich!

Jim McEwan immediately set to in getting the work force brought together under distillery manager Duncan MacGillivray, an Ileach from Kilchoman who had been involved at the distillery before. In 1973 he joined the Bruichladdich Engineering Co. and a year later he was employed by Bruichladdich Distillery as a stillman-cum-engineer-cum lorry driver. Four years later he was promoted to brewer but by the time I visited in 1984, he had left to set up his own garage business as the short time working impacted on the distillery. In 1990 he returned as brewer before Bruichladdich's eventual closure in 1993. The next eight

The new still house takes shape at Caol Ila, 1974.

years were spent with D&N Mackenzie, the local VW dealership as service manager before Jim's call to arms in February 2001. The brief was challenging … the distillery was to be opened during the Islay Festival in late May … 2001! The amount of work that was put in by the assembled workforce was staggering as the buildings were cleared of clutter and spruced up with the new company colour – a turquoise blue reflecting the colour of the water of Loch Indaal. No hi-tech equipment was to be installed: everything was to be done the old-fashioned way. Distilling was recommenced and as the first spirit ran from the stills Jim and Duncan stood silently in front of the spirit safe praying that it would all come good. 'I was desperate to get the heart of the run,' recalled Jim, 'and all I could think of was the amount of money riding on this moment. It was like looking for diamonds in coal dust! But the heart came at last and Duncan and I were so emotional we could not look at each other for fear of bursting into tears.'

With distilling back on song, the re-opening on 29th May was held on a gloriously sunny day during the Feis when people from all over the world descended on Islay to celebrate. Tours both informal and formal were conducted throughout the day, drams and food were dispensed in the courtyard, music filled the air and whisky writers were everywhere. Old friends came by including Iain Allan, who was manager at the time of my first visit in 1984. To mark the event, we were allowed to fill our own 50cl Valinch with a specially selected 30-year-old malt which was wax-sealed on the spot and signed by Jim.

In the evening a ceilidh was followed by a fireworks display the likes of which Islay had never seen before as £10,000 of pyrotechnics went off in the midnight sky over Loch Indaal.

Almost everyone involved in distilling on Islay seemed to be there including John MacLellan of Bunnhabhain who thought it was a 'magical evening' and perhaps wished that as much attention could be lavished on his own distillery. Bunnahabhain's ownership had remained essentially intact since my

visit in the mid-80s. Highland Distillers were the owners until April 2003 and that company is part of The Edrington Group which is in turn part of The 1887 Group, a joint stock company owned 70% by Edrington and 30% by William Grant & Sons. Its future seemed assured and as a major component of Black Bottle blended Scotch, a brand that was in resurgence until recently, it looked as though the truly bad old days were gone for good. But the owner's lack of commitment to the distillery became evident when it announced the sale of the distillery and the Black Bottle brand to Burn Stewart Distillers, the operators of Tobermory and Deanston distilleries. Given that Bunnahabhain's sales budget for 2002 was exceeded by 42% and that this represented a 36% upturn in turnover, one can't help thinking that the sale might be something to regret.

Caol Ila is now in the Diageo stable and is a solid part of the company's malt portfolio. The Hidden Malts range of bottlings released by Classic Malts in May 2002 shows that Diageo have faith in their lesser-known distilleries such as Caol Ila, Clynelish, Glen Elgin (always a crack whisky) and Glen Ord. These are all bottlings that fly in the face of some of the more exotic 'finished' expressions that have emerged in the past five years and appeal to the traditionalist as they have been made in the old-fashioned way with no tinkering in the maturation process. Billy Stitchell is in charge here and can lay claim to being gainfully employed all his life on Islay, a hard thing to do these days! Born at Bunnahabhain, Billy's family have been at the sharp end of whisky production for generations and there is no better example of someone who has the job in his veins. It was from Caol Ila that I embarked on the square-rigger *Jean de la Lune* in July 2001 for the Islay to Skye leg of the Classic Malts Cruise. Sipping a dram of Caol Ila and enjoying fresh seafood on Billy's 'balcony' overlooking the boats in glorious sunshine takes some beating and I recalled that first dram Grant Carmichael poured in the office some 16 years before … there is simply no better place to sample a malt whisky than at its home.

CHAPTER FOUR

JURA

THE FIRST decade of the 19th century brought a contrast in the development of the whisky industry on the mainland and in the islands. The Lowland distillers expanded and increased their output, much to the delight of the Lowland farmers. They were therefore better placed, not only to further increase their share of the massive London market, but also to help satisfy a government hungry for revenue to support the war against revolutionary France.

After a lengthy review of the industry in 1797, the government increased the licence fee for a Lowland still to £108 per gallon of still volume. The large, shallow stills that they used enabled a rapid distillation technique to be employed and the licence fee was calculated on the assumption that a Lowland still yielded 2,025 gallons (9,190 litres) of spirit (pretty awful stuff in practice) per gallon of still volume. Any variance above or below this quota resulted in a tax of 3s per gallon. At the same time, weaker washes resulting in better quality spirit were enforced. To cap it all, a duty was imposed on all wash made and all spirit produced while the distillers were still obliged to give 12 months notice to supply the English market.

In the Highlands and Islands the distillers got a different deal with lower taxes imposed on malt prepared from the lower yielding local barley, the duty on still volume remaining unchanged. Despite these regulations, the Lowland distilleries prospered and revenue rose dramatically. A series of appalling harvests precipitated a total ban on distilling in 1801 and 1802, and the decade closed in similar fashion with prohibition from 1809 to 1811. Against this background of hardship, legal distilling on Jura started up in Craighouse around 1810.

At that time, Napoleon's influence on the continent was also having a marked effect on the whisky industry, in that there was an almost constant shortage of imported grain, forcing the more remote distilleries like Jura to rely on modest supplies of local barley. The war also began to have an effect on the drinking habits of the gentry. As brandy became scarce, whisky grew in popularity but this trend was not apparent in the fortunes of the industry following another rise of duty in 1814.

Prior to 1810, distilling around Craighouse was reputedly carried out in a cave until a rudimentary distillery was erected nearby on the site of the present buildings. Local knowledge has it that David Simson who worked the Bowmore Distillery in the latter part of the 18th century may have been one of the early distillers at Craighouse before the laird, Archibald Campbell decided to rebuild the operation.

The 'Long Road' follows Jura's eastern shore as far as Ardlussa.

The new buildings included maltings, which helped to produce a characteristic peaty malt whisky – a far cry from the current product. Records show that, in 1831, the first recorded licensee was William Abercrombie, who turned the distillery over to Archibald Fletcher the following year. It then remained in the hands of the Fletchers for the next 20 years.

When Archibald Campbell died in July 1835 his estate passed to his son Colin, who also inherited his father's problems. The estate inventory showed that rent arrears to Martinmas (11 November) 1835 amounted to £2,794 6s 8d, of which £2,245 was deemed 'recoverable'. Peter Fletcher was listed as a tenant in Craighouse and the distillery, then known as the 'Small Isles', owed £30 for some 20 weeks rent, though this didn't compare with the new laird's financial obligations – he had owed his father over £17,000 when he died!

Money matters apart, Campbell was soon at loggerheads with his Islay namesake, Walter Frederick, just as his father had been. This time the argument was not over the disputed drove roads through southern Jura, but the high levies on the Port Askaig to Feolin ferry, and in 1839 he registered his protest in court. By the time the Fletchers gave up the lease of the distillery, there were only 1,200 gallons (5,450 litres) of malt whisky in bond on the island and its reputation appeared to have been in question. In December 1851, the factor Neil MacLeod wrote to Richard Campbell who had succeeded Colin to the estate:

As I was leaving the small isles, [he] gave me a sample of his best aged whisky, which I have seen compared at Portaskaig with Caol Ila by the manager Mr Dain, who I believe knows the business well, and makes the best aqua in Islay. I could not get him to express himself as to whether Jura could be improved or not, he merely

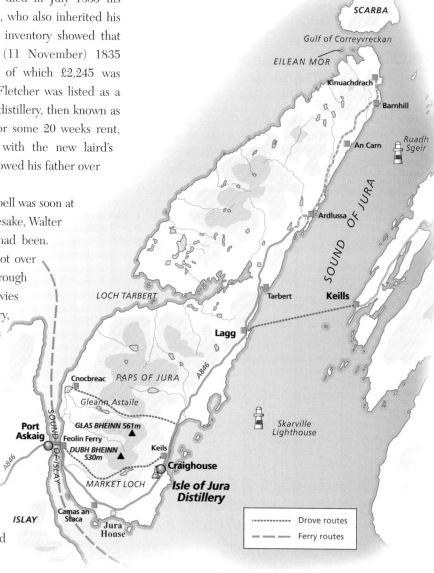

said, old or new it retained its former taste. I believe on the whole the whisky is rather better ...

The distillery passed into the hands of J&A Gardner (or Gardinner) in 1852, but almost immediately there were problems. The Gardners quit, leaving Campbell with the option of selling off the plant for scrap, or finding another distiller who was prepared to take over production at such short notice. Valuations on the brass and copper content of the plant amounted to £400, with the entire contents of the distillery coming to £600, but the valuer felt that realistically only £400 could be raised if it was all sold for its intended purpose. The dilemma was resolved when Campbell was approached by Norman Buchanan of Glasgow, and after some customary haggling a lease was agreed at £90 per annum for five years and £110 per annum thereafter. This included the 'use of the utensils', with the tenant compensating for any reduction in their value at the end of the lease. The laird agreed to supply Buchanan with all the peat he required and assurances were given that all the draff would be taken up by farmers on Jura and Islay.

If you want to travel to Barnhill, you'd better go by 4x4 (upper); Jura Distillery sometime in the 1940s (lower); the Gulf of Corryvreckan (below).

Buchanan entered the distillery in April 1853, around the same time he took over Caol Ila Distillery, which, despite its reputation had been without a licensee since Henderson Lamont & Company had gone bust the previous year. Ten years later Buchanan's business went the same way and the next operators of Jura Distillery were J&K Orr from 1867-1872. Only in 1876, when James Ferguson and Sons of Cadogan Street, Glasgow took over, did Jura enter a period of relative stability, although it was ultimately to end in acrimony between tenant and laird.

Richard Campbell's estate passed to James Campbell, who arranged a lease for 34 years from Whitsunday 1884 in which he made sure that the new tenants of the

The Ferguson family, who eventually quit Jura Distillery in 1901 (upper); the manager's house is just visible on the right and still stands (lower); the old maltings prior to demolition in 1961 (bottom).

distillery undertook to improve the facilities at Craighouse. He did this by binding them 'at their own cost and expense, to erect and completely finish a good substantial pier, with a depth of not less than ten feet of water at the pier-head at low water,' and to 'erect a waiting-room and store on the pier, with road access sufficiently wide to allow two loaded carts to pass at any point,' and a bridge wide enough to take one cart.

The Fergusons must have sunk a considerable amount of money into Jura – the improvements to the distillery alone cost some £25,000. This accounted for four washbacks of 13,000 gallons (59,000 litres) each, a 6,650-gallon (31,200-litre) wash still and two spirit stills of 2,350 and 1,200 gallons (10,670 and 5,450 litres) capacity producing 180,000 gallons (817,200 litres) of spirit per annum.

In 1901, James Campbell died and was succeeded by his son Colin. At the same time the Fergusons quit Jura Distillery, stripping it of all the plant and machinery which they had installed at the start of their tenancy. Their reasons for leaving are obscure, but most sources feel that they were in dispute with the laird. Some correspondence of 1895 between James Ferguson and James Campbell concerns fencing which had been erected by Campbell around the distillery and roadway down to the pier, which Ferguson described as 'at best useless', beseeching him to take it down.

The bonded whisky was removed gradually to the mainland, and in 1905 there was sufficient need for an Excise officer's house to be built at a cost of £869 8s 7d. The Fergusons continued to pay rent up to the expiry of the lease at Whitsunday 1918 when the pier, access road and bridge became the property of the laird. By this time the Fergusons had more or less washed their hands of their interests on the island. The last whisky had left for the mainland in 1913 and they had not bothered to pay much heed to the upkeep of the pier – at least according to Campbell.

Prior to the expiry Campbell had a survey of the pier

carried out by G Woulfe Brenan of Oban who set the extent of the repairs at £1,293. The Fergusons felt that £67 was closer to the mark and the stage was set for another confrontation.

The Fergusons steadfastly refused to pay for the repairs and in October 1920, Campbell instigated legal proceedings against them only to find that George Ferguson had been dead for some time, and James Ferguson was to die soon after the action was served. Upset with the whole affair, Campbell had the roofs removed from the distillery buildings' to avoid paying the rates on them and pursued the Ferguson's trustees. In December 1920 he sued them for £2,793, which included £1,000 for the dredging of the pier-head,

The new Jura stills being unloaded after their journey.

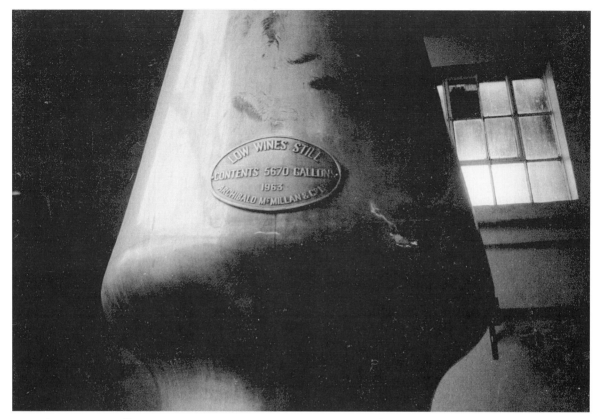

One of Jura's spirit stills.

where the water depth Campbell claimed was less than ten feet at the termination of the lease. If this argument was ever resolved, no record of it exists, but the Fergusons had a very belligerent attitude to the whole affair and were clearly in no mood to settle. In any case, distilling as a viable industry was, for the time being, finished on Jura.

The reasons for the reconstruction of Jura's Distillery in the early 1960s are, thankfully, better recorded. As an island Jura was subjected to the social and economic pressures common to any isolated community. Both war and the drift of the young to the industrial heartlands had reduced the population to around 150 in the late 1950s. Visitors to the island were usually there to stalk the deer that existed in their thousands. George Orwell commented bitterly on the 'deer forest' during his stay at Barnhill in the north of the island. The way in which 'everything is sacrificed to the brutes' did not impress him.

It was Orwell's landlord, Robin Fletcher, along with Frank Anthony Riley-Smith, the owner of Jura estate in the south of the island, who responded to the worsening situation by embarking on an ambitious plan to rebuild the distillery at Craighouse, in the hope that new blood would be attracted to the island. Fletcher was very much the mover and shaker with Riley-Smith owning the land on which the distillery was sited. With financial backing from the brewers Scottish & Newcastle through their subsidiary Waverley Vintners, they recruited Bill Delmé-Evans, who had designed and built Tullibardine Distillery in 1947-8, and gave him free rein over the design. Even Delmé-Evans followed in the island mould as a farmer and distiller, and with a thorough understanding of the value of limited ground, he set about putting the hillside site to the best possible use. There was no constraint placed on the type of whisky that he wanted to create and at the outset a Highland-type malt was envisaged to set itself apart from the neighbouring Islay malts.

'My primary aim was to construct an economic distillery within the space available,' Bill recalled. 'Everything had to be simple and fall to hand. You could not afford to complicate things in so remote a location. I also had to play mother to the large number of incomers on an island without any policemen – some Saturday nights became quite interesting!' The original concept was for 250,000 gallons (1.14 million litres) per year from two stills, the design of which was crucial to the taste of the new Jura malt. 'It was our intention to produce a Highland-type malt differing from the typically peaty stuff last produced in 1900. I therefore designed the stills to give spirit of a Highland character, and we ordered malt which was only lightly peated.'

The weather was a factor over which Bill had no control, so the boats bringing plant and machinery to

An aerial view of the distillery.

Craighouse were frequently delayed. The *Lochard* was often employed on these supply runs but was restricted by having only a 10-ton lifting derrick and therefore much of the plant had to be brought over in sections and built up on site.

Starting up a distillery involves an element of risk, as the quality of the malt whisky can only be discovered when it has matured. In Jura's case the risks were lessened simply due to the fact that the water supply was of known quality, so one of the most essential ingredients was right from the start. Today's commercial distillers can order top quality malted barley to their precise specifications and along with controlled mashing and fermentation the only real unknowns are the water, the shape of the stills and how the process is managed. In 1968, Bill had seen another of his creations come on stream – the Glenallachie Distillery on Speyside, 'but it had taken me three years on my own to find a suitable water source.' Jura's water came from the trusted Loch a'Bhaile Mhargaidh (Market Loch) lying at 800 feet (244 metres) in the hills behind Craighouse.

The distillery was opened by Lord Polwarth of the Scottish Council on the 26th April 1963, and became a major employer on the island. Many of the workforce were recruited from the mainland and encouraged to settle in Craighouse, but inevitably some could not reconcile themselves to the island way of life and left Jura after a while. However, the belief that the distillery

Bill Delmé-Evans, creator of the new Jura Distillery.

would inject new life into the island and bring about an increase in the population proved to be correct – it gradually increased to around 250 in 1985, 11 of whom were employed in the distillery.

Bill Delmé-Evans oversaw these changes as managing director of the distillery company until 1975, when he retired. The company was by then economically sound enough to undertake a self-financing expansion programme over the next three years. In 1976, under the new MD, Dr Alan Rutherford and his manager Don Raitt, the new boiler-house was built and the old gravity-feed system in the filling store replaced with a more modern pneumatic

type, which performed the job in much the same way as a petrol pump. The following year, the stillhouse was extended with another pair of stills, new condensers, feints receiver and spirit safe. A 20-ton wet draff tank was installed along with a new draff drier designed to handle all the draff produced at a projected output of 750,000 gallons (3.4 million litres) per year.

Building of a new dam at Market Loch was started in 1977, but after several unsuccessful attempts to get materials up to the loch by Land Rover, the work was put off until the next year when a helicopter solved the problem. The final push to complete the programme involved the raising of the tun room roof and installation of a centralised electrical control system for the mash house and tun room.

The old cast iron mash tun was dismantled and

Isle of Jura Distillery

Craighouse, Isle of Jura, Argyll PA60 7XT
Tel: 01496 820240
Fax: 01496 820344
www.isleofjura.com
Owners: Kyndal
Manager: Michael Heads

I FIRST MET Michael Heads in 1984 on a visit to Laphroaig when the manager Murdo Reed ensured that he was on hand to cut some peats for our photographer during the original *Scotch and Water* foray. Since then, trips to Jura have been infrequent and my itinerary during the Classic Malts Cruise of July 2001 meant that after leaving Caol Ila we headed due north up the Sound of Islay to sail up the remote western shore of the island. This aspect of the island I

had wanted to see for some years as it is only experienced from the sea. Remote does not do it justice. If you ever feel like getting away from the human race for a few days then a trek up this side of Jura would ensure that you would probably only encounter wild goats, red deer, golden eagles and the occasional adder!

Despite the effort required to get to Jura, it remains one of my favourite distilleries primarily for its very ethos. Its history is about making malt in difficult circumstances and about how a small island community can rebuild part of its past and improve upon it. Latterly it has been all about brand-building with unique expressions such as the Isle of Jura Superstition. This innovative bottling marries aged Jura malts with an Islay-style peated Jura distillation which is supposed to evoke the notion that peat is a life-affirming resource on the island, but one that was traditionally never harvested until May and not a day before.

Another noteworthy factor about Jura is evident from its website. It is very much part and parcel of the community, sharing ideas and news, developing projects and acting in a proactive manner to the benefit of resident and visitor alike. And that is exactly what the island distilling communities in the 19th century used to be.

removed, replaced by a 20-foot diameter stainless steel semi-lauter tun, in order to increase the efficiency of the mashing. The six corten steel washbacks, which became subject to pitting after prolonged use, were also replaced with stainless steel versions of double the capacity. An important addition to the cleansing equipment was the installation of an in-house flushing system utilising all the existing pipework to wash out the tun liquor tanks and washbacks after use. Further plant was renewed with a large oak spirit receiver from Marchive Fruhinsolz of Jarnac, France, installed by Joseph Brown of Dufftown and the malt intake was increased to 30 tons per hour.

Did all these improvements make a better distillery? A more prolific one certainly, but only when everything was working properly which, as the manager in 1984 John Bulman stated, did not happen all the time. Something of the simplicity which Bill had built into the original plan had gone by then, even though the distillery was operating on two men per shift. The result was that John had become a jack of all trades, having to sort out all sorts of teething troubles to get Jura operating consistently, but that was something of which Bill Delmé-Evans as a farmer, architect and distiller would have approved.

In 1985 Isle of Jura Distillery was taken over by the Invergordon Distillers Group who were then subject to a management buy-out some three years later. In 1995, they were in turn absorbed into the Whyte & Mackay empire, part of American Brands. Despite the threat of closure, Jura remained in production under Willie Tait's management throughout the 1990s with Willie also crossing the Sound of Islay to keep a watchful eye on Bruichladdich. Under the auspices of American Brands' Jim Beam Brands (Greater Europe) plc, Whyte and Mackay struggled to perform according to its owners' expectations and in October 2001, the company was bought out by its management for £200m. Willie eventually left to take over at Old Fettercairn in Kincardineshire with Michael Heads leaving Laphroaig to manage Jura.

Managing such a remote distillery creates many unique problems. The new EC regulations concerning

The stillhouse, 1984.

effluent discharge from distilleries is more acutely felt in Islay and Jura than elsewhere and considerable outlays have had to be made to meet this new legislation. Effluent from the Kildalton distilleries has to be tanked across Islay to be discharged into the fast-flowing Sound of Islay and in Jura's case, the reliance on the ferry service across the Sound of Islay is paramount. In June 2002 Michael was forced to send a bill to Argyll and Bute district council for £225,061 which represented the quantifiable losses incurred by Kyndal due to the inefficiency of the new Serco Denholm operated ferry *Eilean Dhiura*. There is no doubt that Kyndal will continue to see Isle of Jura through these frustrating times and hopefully a better and more suitable ferry service will eventually be provided, but as Michael stated at the time, 'If it wasn't such a financial burden, the fact that Isle of Jura whisky travels around the world, but often fails to make the 800-metre journey from Jura to Islay would be laughable.'

Either way, if you're staying on Islay it's worth 'risking' the crossing to take in the distillery.

CHAPTER FIVE

MULL

BOWMORE'S creation as a purpose-built village was reflected in 1788 when Tobermory was established on the shores of 'one of the best natural harbours in Great Britain … ', as reported by John Knox in 1786 to the subscribers of the British Society for Promoting the Fisheries of Scotland. The society was formed to establish fishing communities on the West Coast and to exploit the vast stocks of herring, cod, ling and salmon that lay offshore.

Knox went on a fact-finding mission to reconnoitre possible sites for these communities and submitted his observations to the society, which consisted, incidentally, largely of West Coast landowners and other men of substance. The governor, needless to say, was the omnipresent Duke of Argyll, who happened to own a great deal of Mull.

Knox was an enthusiastic but somewhat naïve observer and was none too impressed by the farming standards he witnessed on his journey north to Mull:

Of grain, this coast cannot raise, with the greatest exertions, a sufficiency for the use of the inhabitants; and of every year's production of Barley, a third or fourth part is distilled into a spirit called whisky, of which the natives are immoderately fond.

He arrived in Oban and found that his transport to Mull had not materialised, but he was fortunate to befriend 'two brothers, of the name Stevenson, who are traders in that place, and to whose industry, that whole district is under great obligations …', who,

'seeing my situation, readily offered to accompany me up the sound, in a new vessel of their own, lying in the bay.' Needless to say, this would have been John and Hugh Stevenson, the founders of Oban Distillery.

The offer of a lift up the Sound of Mull was to prove invaluable to the Stevensons who must have impressed upon Knox their ability to be of use to the society in the future construction of any settlements in the area. Meanwhile Knox recorded that, 'There is not, in this large island, any appearance of a regular well built village, or of manufactures or even spinning to any extent.'

The sheltered bay of Tobermory made a big impression on him, however, and he even went on to suggest to the Duke of Argyll that, 'docks might be formed for building Ships of War. This harbour might indeed be employed by government as an Arsenal for the facilitating of naval equipments and military embarkations in Time of War for America and the West Indies.'

In his submission to the society, Knox proposed that 40 fishing stations should be established along the West Coast. These stations would ideally consist of 16 houses for tradesmen, schoolmaster and innkeeper, erected at a cost of £80 each and 20 houses for the fishermen, at a less substantial cost of £25 – in other words, single storey and thatched as opposed to two storeys and slated. His oversimplified calculations added up to £80,000 being expended on the entire 40 stations. The secretary of the society, John Mackenzie, criticised Knox's assumption that so many stations

Tobermory's colourful frontage.

could be established and remain commercially viable and the decision was eventually taken to establish four stations at Tobermory, Ullapool, Lochbay and Creich.

The duke expected some '30 years purchase of the present rent' for Tobermory from the society which placed advertisements in leading journals for tradesmen and fishermen to petition them for situations in the new villages. This democratic gesture was somewhat tempered by the duke's guidelines to the society's agent (and his own factor) on Mull, James Maxwell, to whom he wrote in May 1788:

In fixing settlers I would have you privately give some attention and preference to such as are considered friendly to my family, but not to the exclusion of any person of real merit whatever they may be in other respects …

Adding that on Mull he had been approached by a smith and a carpenter with offers for rentals, and that 'they had good characters, one of them was a Campbell.' This reference on behalf of his namesake was proffered despite his continuing:

No artificer should be settled unless known good workmen and persons of good character: such as have been bred in Mull or such remote places, unless of some extraordinary merit should not be accepted.

Construction started in 1788 with much of the work being carried out by the firm of Knox's acquaintance John Stevenson of Oban who was responsible for the breastwork built along the high-water mark.

The tenants started to move in as their houses rose around them and by 1792 the customs house was

The Wash Act of 1784 had obliged distillers to take out a licence, and prohibited more than two stills operating in a parish at any one time while restricting the amount of barley consumed for this purpose to 250 bolls per still. No sign of any such distilling within the village (now with a population of some 300 people) was apparent, although the local minister had observed much activity outwith Tobermory, reporting that until:

The late act ... the manufacturing of barley into whisky, was by much too common a practice in this country; but the number of stills have, since that period, been greatly diminished, much to the advantage of the country, and, it is thought, without any loss to the revenue.

established to cope with the traffic Tobermory was then handling. Between 5 April and 10 October 1792 some 1,829 tons of kelp, mostly bound for the glass and soap factories of Greenock and Liverpool, were cleared for export along with 1,070 tons of British salt, 15 tons of lead, 120 cwt of wool, 53 barrels of herring, 17 barrels of salmon, and 46 cwt of cod and ling. At the same time 1,055 gallons (4,840 litres) of wine, 3,575 gallons (16,232 litres) of 'British spirituous liquors' and 659 gallons (2,994 litres) of the foreign variety (ie, brandy, claret, and genever) entered the port. Clearly Tobermory was thriving.

At this time two licensed stills existed within the parish, already well supplied by the imported spirits.

The village was growing steadily – the rent rolls show that the boatbuilder and cooper shared a shed rent-free, while a smith, a wright and various other tradesmen had taken up lots. Another tenant was John Sinclair, a merchant, taking several rentals over a number of years and applying in April 1797 to the society:

To take a lease for 57 years of 80 feet in front and 90 feet backwards of vacant ground at Ledaig. To build stone and lime houses on the front ground and office houses on the back ground, and to make a cut from the Burn or River. As Mr Maxwell thinks the Society cannot alienate so much ground below the bank [Mr Sinclair] is willing to renounce the lease after 10 years possession at 12 months notice ... [Mr Sinclair] will build [at a cost] not exceeding £300 ... [and] expects grass for a horse and moss for two fires.

Although the word 'distillery' at no time appears, the society's answer on 16 May showed that they had clearly discerned Sinclair's intentions:

Duart Castle, Mull, the ancestral home of the Macleans of Duart

Declines proposal of John Sinclair for erecting a distillery at Tobermory. If it will suit Mr Sinclair to erect a brewery the Society would second that idea more readily.

This proved to be only a temporary setback for Sinclair who was establishing himself as the settlers' spokesman. Sometime in 1798 the society gave in to his request and he built his distillery. There appears to be no record of how he changed the society's mind, although in his original offer he mentioned that he would 'provide the fish cures with a sufficient cellar for containing salt.' Perhaps he eventually made them an offer they could not refuse.

In his first year of operation he produced 292 gallons (1,326 litres) of spirit from stills which by law had to be between 30 and 40 gallons (136 and 182 litres) in volume, so he clearly maintained his distillery as a secondary means of occupation to that of merchant.

His grain supplies would almost certainly have come in from surrounding districts or by import, for the ground surrounding Tobermory was extremely barren and much of the society's correspondence at this time dealt with requests for extra pasturage from settlers who universally complained of the rent. Eventually, in 1801, the Duke of Argyll took a rental from MacLean of Duart for the tack of Calve Farm, which included Calve Island at the mouth of Tobermory bay, to alleviate the problem. Some 18 sublets were then created for tenants – one of whom, inevitably, was John Sinclair.

He never seems to have missed an opportunity to consolidate his business in Tobermory. He had a fleet of trading ships working between Glasgow and Liverpool, no doubt carrying a great deal of the kelp produced in the Hebrides, and he even managed to issue his own local currency. His notes bore the following promise:

Tobermory, Island of Mull, 9th January, 1825. For want of change, I owe you five shillings and for four of these tickets I will give you a £1 note – John Sinclair.

The authorities took a rather dim view of all this for in 1826 the promissories were mentioned in evidence before the Small Note Commission. Since 1765 it had in fact been illegal to issue notes of less than 20 shillings value and the fine for such an offence was £500. Even if Sinclair was fined, he was well enough able to pay, since he had in fact retired in 1813 at the age of 43, having made a considerable fortune in the district. He had married into an old Argyll family, the MacLachlans of Rahoy, and started to build up a large estate on the Morvern peninsula around Lochaline. The Argyll Estate sale of 1813 allowed him to purchase the farms of Achnaha, Achabeg, Keil and Knock for £10,000, adding Fiunary, Savary, Achafors and Kinlochaline a few years later. The result being the 8,550 acre Lochaline Estate for the sum total of £20,000, or £2 6s 10d per acre.

Lacking only a residence in which to settle his family he commenced building Lochaline House in 1821, but as it neared completion four years later his wife Catherine died suddenly. With five children to bring up, he concentrated his efforts solely on their welfare and the improvement of his estate and his tenants' well-being. Following his wife's death, he withdrew from the distilling business. With Sinclair's passing, much of the early history concerning the distillery goes too. A succession of licensees over the early 19th century preceded the distillery's closure in 1837, for reasons that are none too clear.

Sinclair continued to live at Lochaline until his death in January 1863 from old age and debility. He had been a generous and philanthropic laird who had never turned anyone from his door and his passing caused great concern in the parish. His granddaughter Agnes King recorded in 1902:

The departure of the family from the house which had been for so long a blessing to the whole district, was a source of distress and lamentation to all, but especially to the poor, to whom it had constantly been an open door of escape in time of need for none were sent away without comfort to mind and body. I cannot forget one old man on the day we left, weeping as he wrung his hands, saying, 'Morvern is a widow today.' In the Gaelic language many of them expressed their sorrow to Mother in words untranslatable – so full of anguish were they – in that most expressive of all languages.

The distillery had gradually fallen into disuse and was entered by John Clark Jnr & Partners of Glasgow after their bobbin manufactory in Salen had burnt down in 1855. They moved the plant machinery up the sound to the distillery where it was stored until it could be set up, but in 1861 two Glaswegian scrap dealers, Duncan Macfarlane and Daniel Murray, broke into the building in an unsuccessful attempt to remove the machinery.

Not until 1878 was the distillery at Ledaig re-established, changing hands twice during the latter part of the century until John Hopkins & Company took over the licence in 1890. The DCL bought them out in 1916, allowing the distillery to operate under the same name. Then, in June 1930, like a great many other distilleries, it was closed and remained silent until 1972.

It still had its uses though, and during World War II the former warehouse at the rear of the distillery was used for naval stores as John Knox's vision of a navy base at Tobermory became a reality. Some 800 sailors under Vice-Admiral Stevenson were harboured in the bay with 200 allowed ashore at any one time. The distillery itself was used as the canteen for a maximum of six ships, while the *Western Isles* lay permanently in the bay serving as accommodation.

Part of the roadside premises has for a long time been used by the Hydro Board as an electricity generating plant which has not helped the problem of good access to the plant. In 1972 Ledaig was purchased from the DCL and re-opened under the ownership of the Ledaig Distillery Limited by a consortium representing Liverpool shippers, later joined by the Domecq sherry group from Spain. The distillery was extensively reconstructed between 1970 and 1972 with output being raised from 350,000 gallons (1.59 million litres) to 800,000 gallons (3.63 million litres).

This doubling of capacity was, unfortunately, to be a major factor in the eventual collapse of the firm in 1975, since it was coupled with the fact that the company had only one major customer who sought other supplies.

Tobermory Distillery

Main Street, Tobermory, Isle of Mull,
Argyll PA75 6NR
Telephone: 01688 302645
www.burnstewartdistillers.co.uk
Owners: Burn Stewart Distillers Ltd
Manager: Alan McConnochie

DUART CASTLE is blessed with one of the most prominent situations of all the island castles. It was restored in the early 20th century as a family home by the late Sir Fitzroy MacLean, the great-grandfather of the current chief, and signals the start of the journey up the Sound of Mull to Tobermory.

On the way up the sound, the ruins of John Sinclair's mansion house lie embedded in woodland, a few miles to the west of Lochaline. The sound turns north-west at Salen leading naturally to Tobermory, which emerges from behind the shelter of Calve Island, as the terraced houses high on the hill above the harbour come into view.

It is easy to see why Tobermory's harbour has for so long been considered one of the best on the West Coast – surrounded by high ground and protected from the swell by Calve Island, it is near perfect for ship and yacht alike, although Samuel Johnson did note in 1773 that ' ... there is a hollow between the mountains, through which the wind issues from the land with very mischievous violence.' Since then trees and town have blended to create a more secure atmosphere, which is enhanced in the evening as the lights of the harbour seduce the yachtsmen and women into the pubs and restaurants ashore.

A receiver was appointed in 1976 and discharged three years later by the Kirkleavington Property Company, which had no previous interest in distilling. Under its subsidiary, Tobermory Distillers Limited, production in 1979 ran to 42 hogsheads (around 6,510 litres) increasing to 575 hogsheads the following year. When I visited in 1984, Tobermory had not produced since, and realistically was unlikely ever to do so. Although a blended whisky had been available under the Tobermory label since August 1980, sales had been largely to the local tourist trade and Tobermory malt had never gained the steadfast reputation within the industry which was and is still enjoyed by the other island malts.

Stock of the blend ran out at the distillery in February 1985, just two months before the manager Alan Jappy and the rest of his staff were made redundant. Efforts to sell the distillery since the autumn of 1983 come to nothing and although production was planned to start up again in April 1984, this too was cancelled. Tobermory's problems were that it not only produced spirit inefficiently but also suffered from poor design, having two tun rooms on

opposite sides of the plant, and no facility for in-house cleansing as exists at Jura. Had these modifications been integrated into a properly designed plant during the reconstruction of 1970-72, then Tobermory might not have waited until 1990 to commence production again. Three years later, Burn Stewart Distillers took over the distillery to add to a portfolio that already included Deanston Distillery in Perthshire.

Gradual investment and development followed, in parallel with the upgrading of the harbour area in the port. Visitors began to come in larger numbers and the reception centre part of the business showed that Tobermory Distillery was being taken seriously as a tourist venue. The tour experience, however, has been criticised as being a bit rushed and suffers from the poor layout of the distillery. Many visitors have commented on the fact that investment can only make things better in this regard.

In 2002 Burn Stewart agreed to a takeover by CL Financial Ltd, the makers of the world-famous Angostura Bitters. This means that a great deal more capital will be invested in the group's drinks interests and I can only hope that some of it trickles down to Tobermory.

In 1984 I recorded that it was unlikely that Tobermory would ever produce malt again, but I had not factored in owner Stewart Jowett's Yorkshire stubbornness and his determination to get the whisky flowing again. He achieved that and more as he was able to negotiate the sale of Tobermory to Burn

Stewart Distillers in July 1993. Having withdrawn from the cut-throat private label bottling sector in 1998 and concentrating on building up their Scottish Leader brand the company was well positioned for a takeover by Trinidad-based CL Financial Ltd in December 2002. The deal valued Burn Stewart at £48.9m and helped to create a significant new drinks group based in Britain with access to worldwide markets.

Returning to Tobermory on the *Jean de la Lune* in July 2001, I had to admit I had got this one wrong as the town was clearly booming with improved pier facilities, numerous restaurants, new bars and extended harbour frontage – none of which was on the cards in the 1980s. John Sinclair would have approved of this new vibrant Tobermory and John Stevenson would have been proud of the way his harbour breastworks have stood the test of time.

CHAPTER SIX

SKYE

CONFLICTING social forces left their mark on the Hebrides in the late 18th and early 19th centuries. The production of kelp from the harvesting of seaweed was one of the most important factors governing the prosperity of the population. During the height of the Napoleonic War the price of this precious commodity (used mainly in the production of glass) was driven to £20 a ton, but out of this sum the kelpers received precious little, with the greater part of the sale price being pocketed by the laird. The Jura historian John Mercer disapprovingly recorded:

The kelpers … were not allowed to work for themselves, but had to pass their produce to the owners, the latter usually paying them about 15 per cent of their own receipts; the kelp left in their chartered vessels, the buyers not being encouraged to visit the islands. The owners benefitted by the increasing over-population, for this meant more kelpers, with the latter's slowly rising incomes allowing parallel increases in their rents. The kelpers were told when and which beds to cut, according to their status in the tenant hierarchy.

However, the tide of emigration to North America gradually rose after the kelp boom, when restrictions on the import of Spanish barilla (which

Hugh MacAskill, founder of Talisker Distillery.

yielded five times more alkali than kelp) were lifted after Napoleon's defeat. Prior to this, the parish of Bracadale in Skye had produced some 50 tons of kelp per year (20 tons of seaweed yielded one ton of kelp), and this modest amount tended to stem the tide of emigration while kelping remained a profitable enterprise for the laird. But, ultimately, there were too many mouths to feed after the war, particularly with 'the return of great numbers of persons formerly employed in the Navy and the Army,' and many appeals were made to the government by the Hebridean landowners whose profits from kelp were diminishing by the year.

The principal Liverpool kelp agents W A&G Maxwell summarised the state of the industry from 1817 to 1828 by calculating that from the sale of a ton of kelp in 1818 at £8 0s 0d, the profit to the landlord was £4 7s 6d after deductions of £2 10s 0d for 'price of manufacture', 13s 0d, for freight, and 9s 6d for the agent's charge. By 1828, a ton of kelp fetched only £3 13s 4d, yielding the landlord just 10d after similar deductions.

Inevitably, many tenants were unceremoniously cleared from the land to make way for the hardy Cheviot sheep – in Skye these clearances were often carried out with little humanity. Many of the emigrants arrived in North America to find that there was little enough room for them, and only the fortunate were provided with ground. Scores never survived the crossing.

In Bracadale parish, many of the crofters were cleared out on behalf of the owner, John MacLeod of Macleod, by Hugh MacAskill of Minginish. In 1821 the parish roll was 2,103. By 1831 it had been reduced to 1,769.

As a tacksman for MacLeod, Hugh MacAskill flourished in the 1820s and 1830s. He was both a sheep farmer and a rent-collector and in the 1820s he was tacksman of Rubh' an Dunain (Rhuadunan), to the south of Talisker, although he extended his holding considerably at a later date. John MacAskill, the Bracadale crofters' spokesman, told the Napier Commission in the 1880s that:

MacAskill had only Rubh' an Dunain in his possession at that time. Glen Brittle was occupied by crofters in comfortable circumstances, and it is likely he asked for Glen Brittle; but, at all events, he got it, and cleared it, and made a sheep run of it. We don't know how many families there were, but at that time there was a church in Glen Brittle, and there is nobody there now to use it. The church is now in ruins, and the manse is converted into a shepherd's house. MacAskill was clearing on the Glen Brittle side, and the doctor [MacLean, of Talisker] was clearing on the Talisker side, from one to the other … There were in Duisdale about a dozen families of crofters in comfortable circumstances. Some of these went abroad, and as Murdo MacKay mentioned, some went to the parish of Duirinish, some to the parish of Snizort, and others to the cities. These clearances were going on under Dr MacLean on one side, and MacAskill of Rhu Dunain on the other. I will take the tack at first. The MacAskills cleared Rhu and a township called Satran, Glen Brittle, Merkadale, Treen, Kraiknish, Brunal, and Brae-Eynort. The people of these townships were scattered through the country,

and some of them went abroad . . . I heard there were sixteen families at one time in Kraiknish, and there is nobody there now but the shepherd. There were ten or twelve in Glen Brittle. There were twenty or more families in Rhu.

By adding up the population of the townships of Satran, Merkadale, Treen, Brunal, Brae-Eynort, and Grula it can be calculated that between 24 and 31 families were evicted by MacAskill in Rhu alone. In total some 250-300 people must have been evicted by MacAskill in Rhu, Kraiknish and Glen Brittle.

Even as MacAskill was clearing the lands, it was calculated that only by abolishing the tax on window glass could the kelp industry be relieved, but by then MacAskill had done the job that the decline of kelp had merely started. The Reverend Roderick MacLeod succinctly described this in the *New Statistical Account of Scotland* as 'throwing a number of farms into one large tack for sheep-grazing, and dispossessing and setting adrift the small tenants.'

In 1825 MacAskill acquired the tack of Talisker House where Johnson and Boswell had stayed with Colonel MacLeod of MacLeod during their visit to the region. Again he evicted many more people and replaced them with sheep – those who remained did so in poverty. The Reverend MacLeod wrote:

The habits of the people are far from cleanly … there were 140 families found in the parish who had no change of night or day clothes … (however, the people) … are shrewd and sagacious, and manifest a good degree of intellect as to the ordinary affairs of life; as to morality and religion, it is yet but a day of small things … (The farming system had) … placed them in such absolute dependence on the tacksmen, as to preclude any hope of amelioration.

Hugh MacAskill was clearly of some means and expanded his interest in 1830 by obtaining a one-acre feu at 30s per annum for 60 years, and a further 20-acre allotment on the shore of Loch Harport at Carbost. His brother Kenneth was by now the bank agent in Portree and was probably instrumental in raising the capital – the considerable sum of £3,000 – which they used to build a distillery on the tack – naturally enough, named Talisker (the name was derived from the 'Echo Rock' or Talamh Sgeir on the shore of Loch Harport). Kenneth was listed as the licensee in 1833, acting as manager and producing malt whisky of good quality with a ready local market. The Rev MacLeod – a passionate, evangelical preacher – upheld temperance zealously and had no doubts as to the effects of dram drinking on his parishioners. In Bracadale were:

… five licensed whisky houses; and whisky is retailed in various other places within the parish, to the manifest injury of the temporal interests of the people, and the progressive and sure destruction of their morals.

Talisker Distillery in its pre-1960 guise.

Scenes from Talisker before 1960.

He went on to conclude his report in a manner which betrayed his bearing in the pulpit:

The most striking variations betwixt the present state of the parish and that which existed at the time of the last Statistical Account, are 1. The formation of a Parliamentary road, which goes nearly over its whole length; 2. The system of farming for some time followed, of several farms being thrown into one grazing; 3. The erection and establishment of a whisky distillery. The first of these variations is a decided benefit to the parish; the second, as decided a disadvantage to its general population; and the third, one of the greatest curses which, in the ordinary course of Providence, could befall it or any other place.

As the MacAskills were in the traditional mould of island farmer-distillers with varying interests, they were able to survive the poor harvests and bad weather which beset the late 1830s and early 1840s causing haphazard production and many distillery closures. Between 1836 and 1843, the consumption of spirits in Scotland dropped from 6.6 to 5.6 million gallons (30 to 25.4 million litres) – 90% of this was malt whisky.

Despite the reputation of its product, on the death of Kenneth in 1854, Talisker was put up for sale at the knockdown price of £1,000, reflecting the depressed state of the malt industry which had continued to suffer from the competition of the large Lowland pot-still whisky producers.

Eventually, in 1863, the year of Hugh's death, the distillery lease was transferred to his son-in-law Donald MacLennan, but his business was sequestrated soon after, and it was not until 1868 that the Talisker lease came into the hands of Anderson & Company. J R W Anderson's business lasted eight years before being dissolved. He was not an entirely honest trader, being found guilty in 1880 of defrauding whisky merchants into believing he had placed whisky in bonded warehouses for them.

Roderick Kemp & Company, in partnership with Alexander Grigor Allan, took over the distillery for just over £1,800 and it was once more in respectable hands. Kemp, on the one hand, was in the wine and spirit trade in Aberdeen, while Allan was one of the owners of Glenlossie Distillery and also Procurator Fiscal of Morayshire.

By 1880 the reputation of Talisker was such that Kemp and Allan immediately started a comprehensive programme of modernisation at a time when Jura Distillery had just been rebuilt. On Islay, Lochindaal was similarly being remodelled while Bruichladdich and Bunnahabhain were just being established. Around the same time the formation of the Distillers Company Limited took place amongst the six major Lowland grain distillers to rationalise competition and regulate prices – their control of the industry was ultimately to reach as far as Talisker.

Alfred Barnard was one of the first to observe the

improvements, reporting the plant contained 'all the newest appliances and vessels known in the art of distilling.' He also recorded that:

Small steamers, or as they are called 'puffers', come up the loch to within 50 yards of the granaries. These bring barley and stores used in the works; and besides this, the 'Hebridean' from Glasgow, a deep sea steamer, calls once a week.

Barnard probably did not witness the loading of casks onto the puffers, and would therefore have been unable to realise the problems that the lack of a pier at the distillery caused. These came to a head in 1891 when Kemp unsuccessfully petitioned his laird, MacLeod of Dunvegan to allow a pier to be constructed, stating that it would be ' … an immense facility for our business.' Ideally Kemp wanted a feu for the distillery so as not to compromise any further investment, such as a pier, that he might make in the distillery. He continued:

When a steamer calls, which most frequently is in the middle of the night, we have to float out the whisky into the loch for a distance of three to four hundred yards, and towed by means of ropes and a small boat in order to get it on board. The difficulty and danger of doing this, especially in a dark and stormy night, no one can imagine except those who witness the operation.
I have no doubt you have heard of the celebrated Glenlivet Distillery which is on the Duke of Richmond and Gordon's land and which is entailed like your own. The distillery has hitherto been tenanted by a lease, but lately His Grace granted the tenant a feu on no other consideration but a very moderate rent for the ground.

After consulting with his lawyer in Portree, MacLeod (who was often abroad in Paris) declined to grant Kemp a feu or the right to build a pier even after Kemp offered to supply all the materials. His

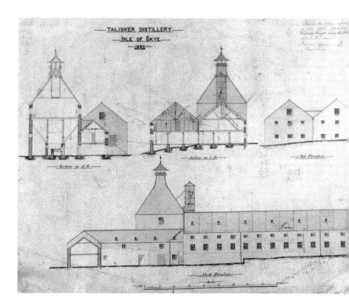

A survey plan from 1880 showing the new kilns and malting floors that owners Roderick Kemp and Alexander Allan had constructed.

correspondence with MacLeod betrayed a growing desperation:

A number of people in attempting to board the steamer in the bay, narrowly escaped perishing. On this occasion we lost a valuable stock of whisky and between 30 and 40 empty casks which were sent to the distillery for filling. Consider the magnitude of this loss alone to us.

Finally he stated that the lack of a pier was ' … paralysing and deteriorating our business to a most serious extent,' and losing patience with MacLeod he sold out to his partner Allan in 1892 when the business was valued at £25,000.

Kemp then bought the Macallan Distillery and Allan took over the business on a leasehold basis (at £110 per annum) with a rent of £23 12s 0d for the surrounding tack and a 10-gallon cask of malt for the laird! It was incorporated in December 1894 as The Talisker Distillery Limited with stock in bond valued at £7,202 in June of that year. An issue of 2,000 preference shares of £10 each and 20,000 ordinary £1 shares was made which were bought up by a wide

Distillery staff c1900.

variety of interests, although Allan retained ultimate control until his death in 1895.

The lease was then transferred by his trustees to the Talisker Distillery Company Limited which operated successfully until 1898 when a resolution to wind it up was passed. This eventually took place in 1900, although by then the company had merged with the Dailuaine-Glenlivet Company to form Dailuaine-Talisker Distilleries Limited. Under Thomas Mackenzie the distillery was extended in 1900, and a pier finally built and connected to the distillery by a railway which is still evident today. At the same time distillery houses were erected for workers and Excise officers, reflecting the trend established at Bunnahabhain, Caol Ila and other distilling communities.

Mackenzie was a capable distiller who had enlarged Dailuaine until it was the largest Highland malt distillery in operation. He was also one of the forces behind the establishment of Imperial Distillery and the associated warehousing at Carron in the late 1890s during the boom in malt production.

(Surprisingly, Imperial was closed in 1899 and did not re-open until 1919.)

In March 1915 Mackenzie died at a time when firms like Buchanan and Dewar were on the verge of amalgamating and the recession in the trade was leading to the merging of many smaller companies with the larger operators. His death led to the eventual takeover of Dailuaine-Talisker Distilleries Limited after the board had approached William Ross of the DCL for advice and guidance.

In 1915 Ross had chaired meetings amongst the leading Highland malt distillers in an attempt to discuss the possibilities of rationalisation amongst them. Despite the failure of these negotiations, the whole of the shares of Dailuaine-Talisker Distilleries was purchased by the DCL, John Dewar and Sons Limited, WP Lowrie and Company Limited, and John Walker & Sons Limited.

This takeover represented one of the first incursions by the DCL into the world of malt whisky production. It was not that they were acquiring a taste for this sector, merely that, under the guidance of

William Ross, they were now administering some sharp medicine to the trade as a whole which would effect a long-lasting cure. Talisker finally entered the DCL fold proper in 1925, effectively making Dailuaine-Talisker Distilleries Limited a wholly-owned subsidiary. The distillery remained licensed to Dailuaine-Talisker until 1930 when operation was transferred to SMD. It was not to experience a change in licensee until 1982, when Dailuaine-Talisker Distilleries Limited was voluntarily wound up and taken over by SMD, transferring the licence to John Walker & Sons Limited whose familiar trademark was inconspicuously introduced to the Talisker malt label, leaving the product's familiar image relatively unchanged.

More fundamental change has altered the distillery since the SMD takeover. Having dropped triple distillation in 1928, the distillery remained unaltered until 1960 when a fire destroyed the entire stillhouse forcing the first shutdown since World War II. Perfect replicas of the five stills were installed as the distillery was rebuilt. These coal-fired items were eventually converted to the more common internal steam-coil heating in 1972 when the malting floors were demolished as malted barley began arriving from the mainland.

The entire distillery, bar the old manager's house, warehouses and offices are post-1960. Despite its apparent youth, one traditional feature has remained intact – the worm-tub condensers. The modern, compact and efficient condensers seen in the great majority of distilleries are absent at Talisker, instead the spirit passes down the lyne arms of the five stills to traditional worm tubs outside the stillhouse. Water carried along a lade from the Carbost burn keeps the tubs brim full of cooling water. It is an archaic feature perhaps, but it never breaks down and gives the visitor a better understanding of the way in which distilleries traditionally operated. Other Diageo distilleries with this type of feature include Royal Lochnagar, Oban and Dalwhinnie.

Talisker is one of the few home-market malts still bottled at a higher than normal alcoholic strength at 45.8% volume instead of 40% and this has lent it an image of being something of a man's malt – robust and strong. Neil Gunn, however, pointed out its only drawback when he said, 'At its best it can be superb, but I have known it to adopt the uncertainties of the Skye weather.'

Nowadays Talisker is a far more consistent product that has won numerous awards in competitions. The 10-year-old has walked off with Best Single Malt Whisky under the age of 12 years at the International Wine and Spirits Competition in 1993, 1997, 1999 and 2001. At the same competition it has won Gold Medals in 1993, 1997, 1998, 1999 and 2001 and at the Monde Selection it has won a Grand Gold Medal in 1995, with Gold Medals in 1993, 1997, 1998 and 1999 along with a Trophy for brands that have won Gold Medals in three consecutive years.

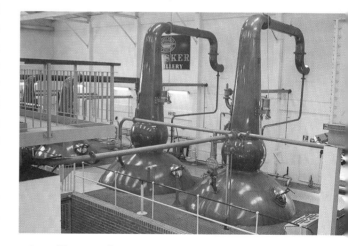

The stillhouse today. Note the downturn in the lyne arms – a Talisker peculiarity.

Most recently in the IWSC 2002, Talisker 10-year-old won the Trophy for Best Single Malt Whisky under the age of 12 years for the fifth time while Talisker Distiller's Edition won the Trophy for Best Single Malt Whisky 12 years and over. The latter expression, finished in Amoroso sherry butts, seems to be the only way that the product displays any variance from the staggeringly successful mainstream trade bottling. But then that is the sort of 'uncertainty' of which Neil Gunn would have approved!

Talisker Distillery

Carbost, Isle of Skye
IV47 8SR
Tel: 01478-640203
Fax: 01478-640401
www.malts.com
Owners: Diageo
Manager: Alastair Robertson

MY ROUTE to Skye in 2001 was slightly less direct than it was in 1984 as the *Jean de la Lune* left Tobermory behind and headed due north past the most westerly point of the Scottish mainland at Ardnamurchan. Far off, the Skye and Rum Cuillin could be seen beyond the low-lying island of Muck, which, as we drew closer, was evidently topped off with a clutch of wind turbine generators. We headed between Muck and Eigg then along the eastern shore of Rum, accompanied by some lively pilot whales, before mooring in Loch Scresort in front of Kinloch Castle, one of the most incongruous constructions anywhere in the Hebrides.

The story of Kinloch Castle is a synonym for the rise of the merchant class in Britain after the Industrial Revolution and the way that they viewed themselves and the rest of the world. Rum was originally owned by the Macleans of Coll who sold it for £26,455 in 1845 to the second Marquis of Salisbury. He did what so many of his class did in those days and promptly created a Victorian highland estate over the entire island by importing red deer and improving the landing facilities by building a pier at Kinloch. Salisbury's eldest son, Viscount Cranborne, then inherited it before the estate passed to his younger brother, the third Marquis of Salisbury.

Farquhar Campbell purchased the island in 1870 and nine years later granted shooting rights to John Bullough, a Lancastrian textile mill owner whose family had been at the heart of the industry that tooled up the mills with mechanical looms. James Hunter Campbell then inherited Rum after the death of his cousin, Farquhar, and it was placed on the market in 1886. Bullough negotiated the purchase of the estate for £35,000 in 1888. Three years later John Bullough died leaving Rum to his elder son from his first marriage, George, who also inherited a fortune of over £500,000 from his father's textile interests. He learnt of his father's death during a two-year world cruise on the family yacht that had been gifted to him and his friends to celebrate his forthcoming 21st birthday. However, there is some speculation as to whether or not this is strictly true as George's father had noticed a developing close relationship with his stepmother, Alexandria, whom his father had married in 1884 and it is thought he was sent packing to keep him out of the way for a while. I tend to favour the latter explanation as George's later indulgences tend to confirm that he had an eye for the ladies.

From this point onwards George (later Sir George) began to spend a large amount of his fortune on Rum in indulgent displays starting with the creation of a Grecian mausoleum at Harris on the south coast of the island to house the body of his father. Deciding that he needed a suitably grandiose base on Rum, in 1897 he commenced construction of Kinloch Castle, completed four years later. Ignoring local advice, he had distinctive (and very porous) red sandstone brought up from Dumfriesshire, thus ensuring years of continuous damp problems for his pet project.

Another of his projects also influenced the design of the castle. George owned the largest private yacht in Britain at that time, the *Rhouma*, and he wanted the façade to match its length of 221 feet (67.3m). Unfortunately two streams running through the site meant that he had to settle for 150 feet (45.7m) instead. This finely colonnaded aspect of the castle was originally roofed in to allow George to go 'jogging' in foul weather.

The castle came with all mod cons. Hydro-electric power came from a dam on the island and the first domestic telephone system in Britain was installed along with elaborate shower baths and a unique electrically-powered Orchestrion (a latter-day synthesiser and one of only two in existence – this one reputed to be a 'cancelled order' of Queen Victoria's) was installed at huge expense.

After George married Monica de la Pasture at Kinloch Castle in 1903, the estate became a playground for Bullough's friends and family with intimate parties being held in the ballroom, the windows of which were set so high in the walls as to prevent anyone from looking in.

The castle gradually filled with treasures from other world trips aboard the yacht as the Bulloughs filled their almost continuous leisure time moving between foreign climes, their Newmarket home and Rum. Unwanted visitors to the island were warned off by discharging shotguns and it soon became known as 'The Forbidden

Kinloch Castle's reception hall, filled with paraphernalia of the Bullough's world travels.

The incongruous sight of Kinloch Castle from Loch Scresort.

Island'. But the Great War stopped all that and gradually their interest waned until they hardly ever visited. Two unwanted visitors who managed to get on to Rum in the early 1930s were Alastair Dunnett and Seumas Adam on their marvellous and inspiring canoe trip up the West Coast. They landed in sight of Kinloch Castle and, as they erected their tent, were immediately asked to leave the island. They refused point blank and were then ordered to go to the castle to discuss the matter with Lady Bullough. They refused again. Later that evening a sheepish house servant returned and asked if they would care to meet Lady Bullough. They accepted but the audience never took place as Lady Bullough felt too unwell. Instead they received her permission to camp and a 26lb-haunch (11.8kg) of venison to boot!

Their stay made such an impression on Dunnett that he recorded it in depth in his book *The Canoe Boys*, describing vividly the way the islanders were forced to live in a social structure of inhibition and denial that was not of their making and he recalled one gathering vividly:

For a long time we retained the memory of a child of this house – a girl of at least 12 years of age, yet so unused to new faces on this desert island that she crouched all the evening shyly behind a chair, peeping and giggling like a four-year-old.

At the time Dunnett and Adam visited, whatever designs the Bulloughs had implanted on Rum some 30 years earlier had withered just as the family's interest had. Sir George died in 1939 to join his father in the mausoleum. The island was managed by trustees until 1957 when the Nature Conservancy bought the whole estate for £23,000 excepting the mausoleum which also accepted Lady Bullough in 1967, aged 98. The whole island is now in the hands of Scottish Natural Heritage (www.snh.org.uk) who maintain it as nature reserve, but one which you are allowed to visit. (Another useful source of information is the Kinloch Castle Friends Association (www.kcfa.org.uk).)

I wasn't sorry to leave Rum but promised to return to investigate its more welcoming charms and we re-embarked to make our way over to Canna and thence to Loch Harport and Talisker.

The conventional road to Skye crosses from Kyle of Lochalsh to Kyleakin (Haco's Strait) on the recently constructed Skye Bridge, near which the Norwegian fleet anchored in 1263, and passes into a region of Skye where Norse associations abound. Although the island is only a short distance from the mainland, it is like another world – the most uncompromising and atmospheric in the Hebrides.

The remains of Caisteal Maoil stand close to the shore where, if legend is to be believed, a Norse princess once levied a toll on passing ships by spanning the strait with a length of chain. This was tethered on the Skye side to a small stone pillar standing on the foreshore about a mile west of the castle and opposite the place where the lighthouse on Eilean Bàn was erected. (This was to be the last home of writer Gavin Maxwell before he died of cancer in 1969.) When the Norsemen eventually quit Skye the

Mackinnons entered the castle under the patronage of the Lords of the Isles.

Maxwell's legacy can be better understood by visiting the Bright Water Centre in Kyleakin and taking the boat trip to Eilean Bàn (www.eileanban.com). Other crossings to Skye are less convenient but offer more flexibility for the visitor: a passenger ferry (www.skyeferry.co.uk) operates during the summer months between Glenelg on the mainland and Kylerhea. This is the point at which Johnson and Boswell crossed, and used to be the focal point of the droving operations for the cattle leaving Skye for the London markets. The current is swift here and the evangelical geologist Hugh Miller described the passage of his yacht *Betsey* through the waters as ' … like a cork caught during a thunder shower in one of the rapids of the High Street.'

Johnson and Boswell, however, had an uneventful crossing, and having disembarked, journeyed down to the ancestral home of the MacDonalds at Armadale, which is now the landing point for the other vehicle ferry crossing to Skye from Mallaig. This crossing offers greater scope for the visitor wanting to explore Sleat, the 'Garden of Skye', and then travel around the flanks of the Cuillins to Loch Harport.

The A851 retraces Johnson and Boswell's route north by Isleornsay (passing by another of Gavin Maxwell's lighthouse purchases) and from there to Broadford and its hotel (the real home of Drambuie) where the A850

Talisker Bay, a window on the Outer Hebrides.

James Boswell, biographer of Samuel Johnson, with whom he visited Talisker House in the late-18th century.

joins from Kyleakin, some eight miles (13km) distant. Before they crossed to Raasay, Johnson and Boswell stayed at Coire-chat-achan in the shadow of Beinn na Caillich (732 metres) and received the same splendid hospitality as a previous guest, the writer and traveller Thomas Pennant. Here, Johnson witnessed the effects of over-indulgence in dram drinking when Boswell was unable to raise himself from his bed until noon the next day.

Johnson, for his part, had become more than a little familiar with one of the married ladies on the previous evening, but it was unlikely that whisky was responsible, for he had only once tried it previously ' … at the inn in Inveraray, when I thought it preferable to the English malt brandy. It was strong, but not pungent, and was free from the empyreumatic taste or smell. What was the process I had no opportunity of inquiring, nor do I wish to improve the art of making poison pleasant.'

He gave a complete record of the Hebridean diet in such a household, and remarked that the man of the house ' … as soon as he appears in the morning, swallows a glass of whisky; yet they are not a drunken race, at least I never was present at much intemperance; but no man is so abstemious as to refuse the morning dram, which they call a skalk.'

They were exposed to a large variety of drink whilst in Skye – including port, claret, punch, brandy, Scotch porter and Holland's gin – but Johnson, according to Boswell, never drank fermented liquor. From Coire-chat-achan, they made their way via Broadford to the island of Raasay as guests of MacLeod of Raasay, where they were received with ' … nothing but civility, elegance and plenty.'

Incidentally, in 1843, Anderson's 'Guide' noted that 'Broadford consists of only three houses and the hotel and the inn, which is a comfortable one. The charges, as in most parts of Skye are moderate. In one article only are they higher than in the mainland highlands, namely, whisky, of which not a drop is made in Skye, either by smuggler or regular distiller.' The author obviously hadn't ventured as far as Carbost, where he would have found the decade-old distillery, and he had most

certainly not bumped into the Reverend MacLeod.

Johnson and Boswell eventually made their way to Talisker by way of Portree and Dunvegan. The present-day road from Broadford continues along the eastern coastline by way of Loch Ainort, before turning down Loch Sligachan where it forks at the head of the loch. The A850 continues to Portree, while the A863 leads through Glen Drynoch to Loch Harport, passing by the ancient burial ground of the MacLeods of Drynoch at the end of the loch. At the turn of the century the Reverent MacCulloch of Portree described it as being 'grisly and gaunt and cheerless, as if a curse rested on it.' The more cheerful prospect of Talisker Distillery lies close to the shore, beyond Carbost village.

The original intended site of the MacAskill's distillery is to be found five miles (8km) further north of the current location at Fiskavaig, just beyond Portnalong, but an unreliable water source forced the brothers to settle for Carbost. A tour around the surrounding countryside is the perfect way to get the most out of a visit to a distillery like Talisker. Over the back of the village some six miles (9.6km) distant, along a bleak moorland road which basks in the grandeur of the distant Cuillins, lies Talisker House where Colonel MacLeod received Johnson and Boswell.

The house is sheltered in one of the most surprising glens in Skye, a gentle bowl hemmed in by steep slopes leading down to the sea presenting a perfect view west to the Outer Hebrides. Johnson, however, saw nothing of the sort and remarked that 'Talisker is the place, beyond all that I have seen, from which the gay and jovial seem utterly excluded; and where the hermit might expect to grow old in meditation without possibility of disturbance or interruption.'

Granted, on the worst of days the place might be foreboding but it seems the perfect spot to end a tour of the Hebridean distilleries; a gentle haven amongst the bleaker surrounding countryside, and one in which Johnson, by his own admission, had never allowed himself to be enamoured of the local spirit – a rule which well over two centuries later the present-day traveller is advised to ignore.

THE MAKING OF MALT WHISKY

A GREAT DEAL has been written about malt whisky, and consequently there is little mystery as to how it is made. But much knowledge has been gained over the years and nowadays the producers are even less secretive than they were in the past and more willing to pass on their knowledge to the trade press, whisky writers and the general public. In particular Diageo, through the company's Malt Advocate programme held regularly at Royal Lochanagar Distillery under Mike Nicolson, has been able to disseminate a huge amount of distilling knowledge not only to their own employees, but also to the likes of myself and other whisky writers.

The basic picture remains the same and despite centuries of constant evolution, malt whisky is still produced in a manner not too far removed from the basic methods employed by the farmer-distillers who developed the industry on the islands in the 18th and 19th centuries. Islay is one of the few places in Scotland where some of the more traditional techniques are still maintained, in particular the process of floor malting can be witnessed at both Bowmore and Laphroaig and perhaps one day at Kilchoman.

Whilst many distilleries receive barley in a ready-malted form to their own specification, of the Hebridean and island distilleries only Laphroaig, Bowmore and Highland Park in Orkney operate floor maltings, producing a proportion of their own malt requirements. None of the mainland distilleries barring Benriach, Balvenie, Glendronach, Glen Garioch and Springbank malt their barley in this fashion any more. Modern malting techniques produce malt of the highest quality more efficiently, but some of the distillery operators clearly believe that by maintaining links with the past the image of their whisky is enhanced whilst the quality does not diminish.

The production of malt whisky is dependent on the processes of germination and fermentation, for the barley

The peat furnace in one of Laphroaig's kilns

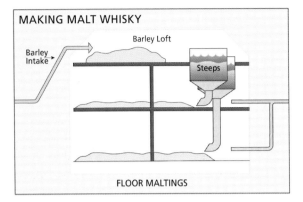

MAKING MALT WHISKY

Barley Loft

Barley Intake

Steeps

FLOOR MALTINGS

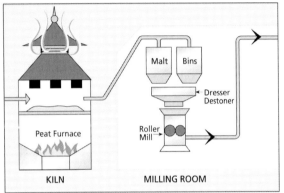

Malt Bins

Dresser Destoner

Roller Mill

Peat Furnace

KILN   MILLING ROOM

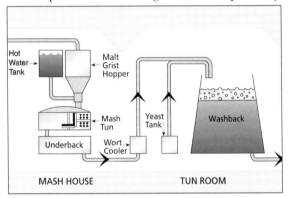

Hot Water Tank

Malt Grist Hopper

Mash Tun

Yeast Tank

Washback

Underback

Wort Cooler

MASH HOUSE   TUN ROOM

Steeping can be witnessed on Islay at Laphroaig, Bowmore and Port Ellen Maltings. The latter establishment was built in 1973 to supply Port Ellen, Caol Ila and Lagavulin distilleries with their entire malt requirements. Such large amounts require fully

must be awakened from being a dormant seed into an active growing plant with a supply of energy-giving sugars from which alcohol, with the aid of yeast, will ultimately be extracted. A grain of barley consists of two main parts: the embryo (from which the living plant will develop); and the endosperm, surrounded by a tough cell wall, which is the starchy energy-rich food store on which the embryo feeds during the early stages of germination.

Germination is initiated by steeping the barley for two days in fresh water which is periodically changed. The island home distillers of the past achieved this by simply placing sacks of barley in a stream for a couple of days, but the requirements of a modern distillery normally dictate the use of large cylindrical vessels, varying in capacity from eight tonnes at Laphroaig to the huge 25-tonne steeps at Port Ellen Maltings. Steeping causes the enzymes contained within the embryo and the cell walls surrounding the endosperm to enter it, thus helping to convert the insoluble starch granules into a more soluble sugar form which eventually aids extraction.

automated processes, in contrast to the smaller scale operations at Laphroaig and Bowmore. At the time of my original journey, Port Ellen was exclusively supplying the DCL units on Islay, but after the Guinness takeover in late 1986 a concordat with the other Islay and Jura distillers was arrived at in 1987 and supplies were extended to them as well.

The steeps at Laphroaig are loaded directly from the barley loft above the floor maltings. Four hundred tonnes of ripe, graded, barley lie in the loft and its quality is critical, for if it is too moist it will go mouldy and won't germinate properly. The barley has a moisture content of around 12% prior to steeping, but when it is emptied from the conical lower section of the steep onto the malting floor this will have risen to around 45%. The barley is spread to a depth of about 4-6 inches (10-15cm); as germination continues the barley is raked and turned by hand to prevent the temperature of the 'piece' exceeding an ideal 15°c.

Depending on the season, the long row of windows on either side of the floor are also used to aid temperature control as the piece is conditioned with hand-turning over a seven-day period. The barley sweetens as the endosperm becomes more sugary in nature, a process which the maltman calls 'modification', the tell-tale signs are the internal development of seedling shoots and the growth of

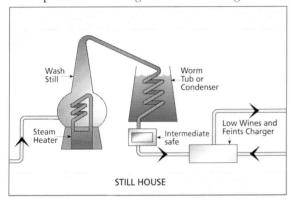

STILL HOUSE

rootlets, which the raking also helps to disentangle.

After steeping at Port Ellen maltings, the barley is dropped by remote control into any of seven huge germination drums of 65 tonnes capacity each. Their size is such that they completely fill the ground floor and main body of the whole plant. As the barley lies on a perforated floor running the length of the drum, up to 17,000 cubic feet of conditioned air is passed every minute through the blanket of barley to effect perfect temperature control. To prevent the growing rootlets and shoots stitching the blanket together, the drums are turned up to three times a day.

After six days in the drums, the barley is in the same condition as on the floor maltings at Laphroaig or Bowmore just before being loaded into the kilns. The grain is now soft and pulpy and further growth must be stopped if the sugars in the endosperm are to be conserved for fermentation. In this condition the barley is known as 'green malt' and is dried at a temperature no higher than around 70°c so as to preserve the vital enzymes that are busy converting the starch into sugar.

In the Laphroaig kilns the green malt, now with a moisture content of 40-2%, is spread to a depth of 12 inches (30cm) and hand-turned with wooden 'shiels' during the two days it lies there. Some 12 feet (3.6m) below the grating on which the malt lies, is the peat

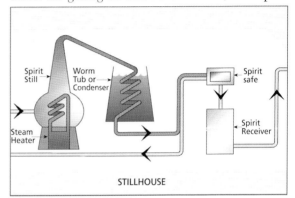

STILLHOUSE

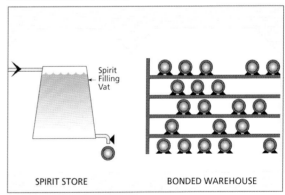

SPIRIT STORE   BONDED WAREHOUSE

furnace. During kilning the constant exposure to the peat reek subtly imparts flavour to the drying malt. At Port Ellen kilning takes around 36 hours, but both here and at Laphroaig heavy fuel oil is consumed to generate hot air for the major part of the drying process, with peat used as a secondary fuel. In some Islay whiskies, however, the peat is of great importance as these whiskies are characteristically heavier in body and flavour than their mainland cousins. The kilns at Bowmore are truly unique in that hot air is blown through the malt from below by fans using heat from a

recycling system. There are also extractor fans above the malt to help to draw the air from below so that the kilning process takes only 42 hours (compared to 48 hours at Laphroaig) and results in three full kilnings being carried out in a working week.

In the past, the home distillers achieved similar results by taking the saturated sacks of barley from the stream or bog-hole and drawing them out to drain until the grain began to germinate. It was then heaved onto a floor, and turned by hand occasionally until the shoots had grown half-way down the near transparent grains. By thickening the piece on the floor, the temperature was raised until it could be detected by hand, at which time it was thrown into a round pile or 'withering heap' for 24 hours or longer. Having been

carried to a kiln the grain was dried by peat over which rotten straw and then a hair-cloth was often placed to prevent loss.

The remains of many such kilns can still be seen on Jura. Although they are officially described as lime kilns, it is almost certain that they were also employed to make malt. An example can still be seen in the nearby wood at the ruins of An Carn, but local knowledge also suggests that it could even have been used to fire an illicit still. These kilns were stone structured bodies commonly 10 feet (3m) across at the base, tapering to a height of four feet (1.2m) where the diameter of the opening was around six feet (1.8m). Within, the walls sloped in to a base some three feet (0.9m) wide where a small tunnel led to the site of the

Left: Laphroaig's current seven-still set up was
created in the 1980s
Top: A malting floor at Laphroaig.
Above: One of the 25-tonne steeps at Port
Ellen Maltings

drying fire on the outside. It was a reasonably efficient – though relatively primitive – method when compared to the modern distillery kilns in which loss through burning is unheard of.

The malt that leaves the kiln has a moisture content of around 3-4% and is therefore noticeably firmer than green malt. It is then stored before use in the next stages of malt whisky production, namely mashing, fermentation and finally distillation.

Both Laphroaig and Bowmore can produce between 20-30% of their total malt requirement in their floor maltings; the remainder arrives in bulk from Port Ellen Maltings. After release from storage the malt is stripped of all dried rootlets and shoots, which conveniently find a ready market as animal feed. The malt itself is ground to a coarse grist by large mechanical roller mills, which aids sugar extraction during mashing. The ancient counterparts of these mills can be found in the rotary querns, or hand mills, that were fashioned from a solid piece of stone, and remained common within the Hebrides until the 1860s when water-powered mills were eventually established.

Mashing can be witnessed at any of the distilleries that are currently in production, but again there are variations on the theme to be found in the islands. The process is carried out in a large cylindrical tank (often 20 feet/6m across) called a mashtun. The more modern canopied tuns are usually constructed of stainless steel, though Bowmore's is of resplendent copper and Bruichladdich's is iron, open-topped and the original article. By peering into any of the island mashtuns, you can clearly see, about six feet (2m) below, a raised perforated floor made up of individual plates, sitting just clear of the bottom of the tun. The grist is premixed with hot water (at about 65°c) and poured onto this floor and the resultant brew is then agitated by an arrangement of stirrers revolving around a central vertical axle. Depending on the efficiency of the mixing and extraction equipment, the capacity of the mashtun may vary.

At Jura Distillery an efficient semi-lauter tun allows two mashes of 4.75 tonnes of malt to be completed in about 9.5 hours. The tun is then drained of fluid (which is retained) and refilled three or four times with increasingly hot water to extract all the residual sugars from the grist.

During mashing the enzymes continue to break down the complex starch molecules into the simpler sugars; the resulting sweet liquor is called the wort. Usually, the first two waters are drained from the bottom of the tun into an underback and the final water returned to the tun as the first water of the next mash, thus helping to maximise the extraction of the sugars. The spent grist, or 'draft', left lying on top of the grating is then removed from the tun and sold as cattle feed to the local farmers.

Fermentation is not quite the simple and phrenetic activity that it appears to be, but a series of complex chemical reactions of which the main by-product is alcohol. All this takes place within the washback, traditionally constructed of pine and resembling an enormous vat sometimes 20 feet (6m) in depth. Caol Ila possesses some of the largest washbacks in Islay, constructed of Oregon Pine, but stainless steel is now being used more extensively. Examples of this type can be seen at Bowmore and Laphroaig.

The wort passes through a heat exchanger to cool it to around 21°c to preserve the sugars of which it is now predominantly constituted. Once this known volume of wort begins to enter the washback a small, but precise amount of living yeast is added, and fermentation commences. The yeast absorbs part of the sugars as food in the absence of oxygen, the end-products being alcohol and carbon dioxide. A system of rotating arms called switchers is usually employed to control the frothing head of the brew as the reactions proceed and the carbon dioxide continues to erupt from the liquid. Fermentation is a violent, seething activity and it is not advisable to peer too closely into a washback for the lack of oxygen can literally take your breath away.

The living yeast multiplies, eventually consuming all the available sugars, and activity then dies down after some 40 hours with the resultant brew or wash containing what yeast is left, water, and around 5-6% alcohol. The wash is then checked by the distillery management to ascertain the yield of alcohol to be expected when it has been distilled.

The compounds that make up the wash all have differing boiling points. The effect of distillation upon them is to separate one from the other so that the desirable alcohols with lower boiling points are extracted first, thus producing spirit. To achieve this, the wash is transferred to the wash stills, which are basically onion shaped, made of copper and usually heated internally by coil tubing conveying steam. As the wash is brought to boiling point the alcohols evaporate first and rise up the neck of the still. They then pass over into the condenser, where they are cooled and liquify, running down into a receiver called the low wines and feint charger. Gradually the proportion of alcohols within the condensate decreases as the amount of water vapour increases. When only pure water vapour is present, distillation is stopped, the product being nothing more than a dilute impure spirit containing about 15% abv – so it must be redistilled.

These low wines are then passed into the low wines

or spirit still and the process is repeated with the more volatile compounds again boiling off first – these are called the foreshots and are sent back to the low wines and feints charger. The foreshots begin to emerge at 90°c with a high alcoholic content of 75-80% abv. When the distillate reaches the required strength it is diverted into the spirit receiver. The integrity of this portion of the spirit is determined by the stillman who makes a series of checks on it. These consist of the specific gravity or density, and also the reaction of the spirit to the addition of distilled water, to proof strength, to a sample. When the mixture stops being cloudy and clears, it is then collected.

These tests are all carried out within the confines of the spirit safe, a glass-walled, brass-bound case through which all the run-off from the stills must pass. The stillman can test and divert the spirit from one receiver to another by turning taps outwith the safe, but he cannot open the safe during distillation as the distillery management hold the keys to the large brass padlocks which secure it. The management submit a return to the Customs and Excise of the amounts of wash and spirit produced – a more relaxed arrangement than that which existed before April 1983 when the Customs and Excise officer measured the yields and held the keys.

The strength of spirit collected varies from distillery to distillery. Diageo, as a whole, have a range from 65-73% abv depending on the particular distillery. As the spirit run continues, a family of aromatics emerges from the spirit. These are the feints and they consist of the heavier compounds and less volatile constituents of the low wines such as fusel oil. Although undesirable compared to the purer ethanol of the middle cut, feints appear (with some elements of the foreshots) in varying quantities in the final product, contributing to the character of each malt whisky. As the run continues, so their intensity increases. At this point, despite the alcoholic strength still being high, the stillman will stop collecting the spirit and divert them either to a feints receiver or charger, or to the combined low wines and feints charger which also contains the foreshots. Depending on how long the feints have been allowed to distil over in the middle cut, the more robust the whisky will be.

The mixture in the low wines and feints charger is re-distilled with the next charge of low wines and the content of the still is then run down to 0.1% abv and is known as the spent lees which is waste. The chemistry of the low wines is complex, as there are literally hundreds of compounds present, along with some that have yet to be identified. They all appear, to a greater or lesser degree, in the whisky that we drink from the bottle. These compounds are collectively known as the congenerics and are responsible for the distinctive nose and flavour of the island whiskies – they help give Laphroaig that hint of seaweed for which it is famous, Bowmore that rich peaty-smoky bouquet and Jura that subtle, Highland freshness.

Other important but lesser known factors are the effects of copper and the temperature at which the condenser is operated. As the distillate is in constant contact with the surface of the condenser, it has a bearing on the finished product. Copper has the ability to 'take out' heavier compounds and in concert with the temperature at which the condensers are operated, the exposure of the distillate to the copper and length of time it comes into contact with it affects the character of the whisky. Generally, if the condensers are run cold, a heavier spirit emerges and the longer the distillate is in contact with the copper, the lighter the spirit will be.

The home distillers and smugglers of the 18th and 19th centuries were able to produce their whisky with equipment and utensils which have recognisable counterparts in all of the existing island distilleries, particularly Bowmore and Laphroaig. Having ground their malt in a hand mill or with the help of an understanding local miller, they relied on a number of casks, usually of 50 gallons (230 litres) capacity, in which they prepared their mash and wash. Fermentation was started by the addition of bub, that is a small amount of barm, or yeast mixed with a little of the wort as a pre-mix and then added to the casks of wash to accelerate the onset of the process. The entire operation was carried out in any convenient farm steading, or in the case of the illicit distillers, in seashore caves or hollows high on the bleak moors. When the Excise did trudge over the landscape in search of the distillers they almost always found the bothies unoccupied. Between May 1837 and January 1844 the Excise working out of Port Ellen seized five stills, 198 bushels of malt (only five of grain), 18 empty casks, 950 gallons (4,313 litres) of wash, four casks of low wines and one malt mill. Most of this was destroyed on the spot – the Officers invariably citing that 'the items were too bulky to remove to Port Ellen', or was it perhaps the thought of that long trek back over the moor? Or perhaps a deal was struck …

Normally the distillate was cooled by running down the neck of the still and passing through a coil, or worm placed in a cask of cold water, known as the worm tub. This feature has gradually given way to the more efficient water-jacket condenser in most modern distilleries, although Mortlach, Cragganmore, Glenkinchie, Dalwhinnie, Benrinnes, Glen Elgin, Oban, Royal Lochnagar and Talisker still employ the traditional method. Another interesting technique was the use of soap during distilling. Samuel Morewood pointed out how important this was:

It is a mistaken notion to suppose that soap is used only by the great distillers, since it is considered an indispensable article by every person who understands the mode of working a still on the old system.

Why was soap used? Simply because it acted as a surfactant and reduced frothing within a still, particularly when it was directly heated by coal or gas. The use of bub died out in the 1960s, as there was found to be more chance of inducing bacteriological infection in the pre-mix. The use of a smaller amount of living yeast has put an end to this.

What then is the destiny of the whisky prior to the bottle? It enters the receiver at the found strength of around 71-2% abv and is normally casked at this strength or at a lesser strength after addition of water, which can be as low as 63.5% abv. The casks come in a number of sizes, each type having an important effect on the maturing whisky – generally, the larger the cask, the longer the maturation time. The casks must be made of oak and be of European or American origin. Oak is ideal as it contains cellulose, hemicellulose (which caramelises thus adding sweetness and colour), tannins which produce fragrance and delicacy and lignin which adds vanilla tones and creates a more complex character. Oak also breathes as the staves are cut across the medullary rays so that oxidation can occur. This removes harshness, increases fruitiness and helps to create a more complex spirit.

So during storage in bond various chemical reactions take place within the cask, the whisky itself changing gradually in nature. The oak wood imparts some chemical components to the whisky and these react to produce subtle changes in the spirit. The very atmosphere of the bonded warehouse can exert an effect as well, as the casks are porous and evaporation of around 1-2% of the contents per annum is allowed for by the Customs and Excise. This, as I am sure you know, is the ubiquitous 'Angels' Share'.

Within the earthen-floored vaults at Bowmore one can sense this relationship as natural moisture seeps from the soil and lies in long pools between the rows of barrels – the temperature is neither warm nor cool, the smell dank and musky. Most of these casks are of American origin, being old bourbon casks that by law can only be used once in their native country.

Some of the cask ends carry the customs stamps and language of Spain with 'Xerez' clearly marked into the wood. These are the ex-sherry butts, traditionally the most ideal in which to mature whisky. The main advantages of the butt are that it is of perfect size (110 gallons or about 500 litres) and also imparts a rich, warm colour to the whisky through the interaction of the spirit with the tight-grained Spanish oak wood. They are invariably preferred to the ubiquitous pre-treated casks that were pioneered by the Glasgow whisky broker W P Lowrie in 1890. He found that by swilling out a new cask with a dark sherry and allowing the wood to soak it up, the whisky emerged resembling the sherried item. A concentrate called paxarete was once in use to this effect, but many distillers and blenders, including Kyndal who own the Jura Distillery, will not pre-treat their casks.

So the whisky lies for the legal minimum of three years, gradually changing in character and composition until such time as it is required for bottling as a single malt, for export in bulk form, or for use in blending. All the island malts are available in bottled form either from their owners or via the independent bottlers. They all differ, some subtly, some not so, but they are all regarded highly and are amongst the most important malts used in blending. It is true to say that very few blended whiskies of the countless numbers available in the world today do not have an island malt in their make-up.

The WP Lowrie cooperage in Washington Street, Glasgow, 1887

THE LOST DISTILLERIES
OF ISLAY

A**S WELL AS** the seven operating distilleries on Islay today there have been a number of other sites where licensed distilling has long ceased. This is an A-Z list of those former locations, who distilled there and dates when they are thought to have operated.

ARDENISTIEL DISTILLERY

(*aka* 'Ardenistle', 'Islay' and 'Kildalton' Distillery)
Established: 1836

OS Map Reference: NR388450

After the successful establishment of Laphroaig Distillery in 1816, a farm tack was leased by Walter Frederick Campbell to James & Andrew Gairdiner, financiers for the Ardenistiel Distillery, who then put it in the capable hands of James & Andrew Stein of the noted Clackmannan distilling family. They ran it until 1847, operating on a site immediately adjacent to the Laphroaig Distillery. Ardenistiel was then assigned to John Morrison, a previously unsuccessful manager of the Port Ellen Distillery. He was unable to make a go of it and only remained until he was sequestrated in 1852. The distillery then passed to John Cassels, of whom little is known and whose tenure at Ardenistiel appears to have lasted for less than a year. It then came into the hands of William Hunter who struggled to make the distillery pay, operating at half capacity producing 33,000 gallons (149,820 litres) a year. By February 1866, William Hunter was made bankrupt and by 1868 the distillery was reported as dilapidated. It was eventually thrown in with the Laphroaig Distillery and its derelict buildings eventually became the site of Laphroaig's warehouses and offices today.

ARDMORE DISTILLERY/LAGAVULIN 2

Established: 1817

OS Map Reference: NR406456

Little is known of the Ardmore Distillery which shared the sheltered bay at Lagavulin with the Lagavulin Distillery. It was established in 1817 by Archibald Campbell, although when the name Ardmore was adopted is uncertain. It opened as a 92-gallon, single-wash-still distillery, but within a year was operating under double distillation with the addition of a 30-gallon low wines still. By 1825 it was being operated by John Johnston of Lagavulin who ran both distilleries simultaneously often using the names Lagavulin 1 and Lagavulin 2. Johnston died in 1836 and in 1837 a valuation carried out shows the two distilleries as having operated during John Johnston's tenancy. 'The Still House (No 2), Tun Room and Malt Barn No 4' were all listed as belonging to the laird Walter Frederick Campbell, as 'Ardmore Distillery'. Alexander Graham, a Glasgow distiller-merchant and owner of the Islay Cellar that supplied Islay malts in Glasgow and to whom Johnston was indebted, acquired the distillery for the sum of £1,103 9s 8d. Lagavulin and Ardmore were immediately merged and together form the site of much of the present-day Lagavulin site.

BRIDGEND DISTILLERY
& KILLAROW DISTILLERY

Established: unknown

OS Map Reference: NR336624

Details of these two (or three) distilleries located at the former island capital, Bridgend, are very limited. David

Simson is on record as operating a licensed distillery at Killarow until 1766 when he moved to Bowmore to establish the distillery that survives there today. Its exact location is unknown. A Bridgend Distillery was custom-built by Donald McEachern Snr in 1818 with a wash still of 146 gallons producing single distillation whisky. It was then run by his son Donald Jnr between 1818-21, when the company was wound up and ceased operations. Information exists that suggests a distillery was licensed to a J MacFarlane at Bridgend around 1821 with an annual output of 3,937 gallons (perhaps a new owner for the McEachern's distillery?).

DAILL DISTILLERY
Established: 1814

OS Map Reference: NR363626

Daill Distillery probably operated as a farm distillery after the Small Stills Act encouraged distillers to go legitimate. The distilling operation was, throughout its short life, in the hands of the McEachern family with the license being held successively by Neil McEachran from 1814-25, Malcolm McEachern from 1825-26 and Donald McEachern between 1826-34. By 1827 it had an annual output of 6,043 gallons of proof spirit. Its demise, like that of many inland distilleries on Islay, was probably sealed by the difficulties of transporting the product to mainland markets. Buildings in remarkably good condition at Daill farm still exist, and these could well have been the location of the McEachern family distilling operation.(see below).

LOCHINDAAL DISTILLERY
(*aka* 'Port Charlotte' & 'Rhinns') Established: 1829

OS Map Reference: NR253585

Lochindaal was a purpose-built distillery in the Rhinns of Islay which survived into the 20th century. Located in the heart of Port Charlotte village it was constructed for its first licensee, Colin Campbell, in 1829. He only held onto it for two years and subsequently it had many owners: McLennan & Grant from 1831-2; George McLennan 1833-5; Walter Graham 1837; Henderson Lamont & Co until 1852; Rhinns Distillery Co 1852; William Guild & Co to 1855 before a period of stability under the ownership of John B Sherriff until 1895 and then J B Sherriff & Co Ltd up to 1921. It was eventually taken over by Benmore Distilleries Ltd in 1921 prior to that company's acquisition by the DCL. That signalled the end of Lochindaal and it closed in 1929. Some of it was used by the Islay Creamery until the early 1990s and the shore-side warehouses remain in use by a local garage and the Islay Youth Hostel and Field Centre, whilst a roadside building is now used for vehicle repairs and the distillery cottage is still inhabited. The bonded warehouses on the hill behind the distillery site have been in continuous use by other distillers and are currently used by the Bruichladdich Distillery. This is the one defunct distillery on Islay that has a good photographic history, which clearly records the distillery site during its century of operation.

LOSSIT DISTILLERY
Established: 1826

OS Map Reference: NR407658

Lossit Distillery was located at Lossit Kennels, not far from Ballygrant on the minor road to Lossit Farm, close to Loch Ballygrant. It was a medium-sized farm-scale operation and in 1826-7 it produced 12,200 gallons (54,480 litres) of proof spirit. It was operated by Malcolm McNeill from 1826 to 1834, by George Stewart until 1852 and a John Stuart thereafter for a further 10 years. This makes it one of the longest surviving 19th-century farm-scale distilleries on Islay. There is a possibility that Bulloch, Lade & Co used the Lossit warehouses (perhaps to store Caol Ila whisky) until 1867. Today the house and kennels remain, although where whisky distilling actually took place remains a mystery and there is nothing left of the warehouses.

MALT MILL DISTILLERY
Established: 1908

OS Map Reference: NR404457

When Sir Peter Mackie lost his bitter legal dispute to retain the sales agency for Laphroaig whisky in 1907 he reacted in characteristic style by deciding to make his own 'Laphroaig' type whisky and in 1908 built a traditional small pot-still distillery within the Lagavulin complex. Despite hiring staff from Laphroaig and attempting to copy the Laphroaig recipe, it did not succeed, perhaps because it used a different water source. Malt Mill tried to replicate a traditional style of Islay whisky, using only peat-dried malt, and it is reputed to have had heather added to the mash. It was always a small-scale operation producing 25,000 gallons of proof spirit (113,500 litres) in its first year, compared with 128,000 gallons (581,120 litres) at Lagavulin. What is perhaps surprising is that it survived

until 1962 when it was merged with Lagavulin and its coal-fired stills moved to the latter's stillhouse for another seven years use. The Malt Mill distillery building is now the reception centre within the Lagavulin Distillery site.

MULINDRY DISTILLERY
Established: 1826

OS Map Reference: NR353594

This is perhaps one of the shortest lived and unlikely distilleries on Islay. Built by John Sinclair in 1826 it operated at a site beside the junction of the Neriby Burn and the River Laggan, next to McNeill Weir (the start of the Bowmore Distillery lade) and its machinery was water-powered from the nearby river. Its output in 1826-7 was 4,332 gallons (19,667 litres) of malt whisky. Sinclair, according to the local Excise officer in 1831, liked his own product a little too much which may account for his bankruptcy that year and emigration to America. The distillery appears never to have reopened and today all that is left is a pile of overgrown stones and a derelict croft.

NEWTON DISTILLERY
Established: 1819

OS Map Reference: NR345624

The Small Stills Act of 1816 encouraged quite a few individuals to take out distilling licences and in 1819 Thomas Pattison opened a farm distillery at Newton, located off the Bridgend to Ballygrant road. Newton produced 6,122 gallons (27,793 litres) of spirit in 1826-7. It operated continuously until 1837, by which time most farm-scale distilling operations had closed on Islay. Little is known about the operation of this distillery although there is still an outbuilding at Newton House that could have been part of the distillery and the metal bars on the windows are perhaps signs of previous use as a bond.

The Malt Mill Distillery Staff with Sir Peter Mackie seated in the centre

OCTOMORE DISTILLERY

Established: 1816

OS Map Reference: NR248589

This farm distillery on an ancient site behind Port Charlotte was run from 1816 until 1840 by the Montgomery family and licensed to George Montgomery. It appears to have operated as a single-still distillery with a wash still of 60 gallons volume (272 litres) with 998 gallons (4,530 litres) of spirit produced in 1817-18, this rose to 3,551 gallons (16,121 litres) in 1826-7. Little is known about its operation until the death of George and his brother around 1840, when it fell into disrepair and the lease was eventually relinquished to the laird, James Morrison in 1854 for £150. Buildings in the farm steading remain today, although some have fallen down and others have been recently been converted into holiday cottages, so guests could well be sleeping with the spirits of 160 years ago! No detailed plans of the distillery buildings have yet come to light.

PORT ELLEN DISTILLERY

Established: 1825

OS Map Reference: NR360458

Port Ellen is fully covered in chapter three, pages 60-67.

SCARABUS DISTILLERY

Established: 1817

OS Map Reference: NR348653

One of the most obscure and short-lived farm distilleries on Islay. A licence was taken out in the name of John Darrach & Co for the year 1817-18. It seems likely that this was a opportunist attempt at distilling following the 1816 Small Stills Act as records reveal a 76-gallon (345-litre) single-still operation in 1817-18. Scarabus Farm still exists (off the Ballygrant road), although whether this was the exact location of the distillery and what happened to it after its two short years remain to be discovered.

TALLANT DISTILLERY

Established: 1821

OS Map Reference: NR337587

This distillery was established in 1821 by the brothers Donald and John Johnston at Tallant Farm, near Bowmore. Excise records until 1827 show this distillery recorded as one of two 'Bowmore' distilleries. It appears to have been a true farm-scale operation with Angus Johnston listed at one point as distillery manager. It was never, however, a profitable commercial operation, perhaps in part due to the generous drams John provided to visiting workmen and farmers. Output was as low as 220 gallons (998 litres) a week and reached 2,101 gallons (9,538 litres) in the year 1826-27. The business folded in 1852, although John's brother Donald and his son, Alexander, were to become successful distillers figuring prominently with Laphroaig's development. Tallant Farm exists today and many buildings from those distilling days remain, albeit some in a state of collapse.

Other Islay locations thought to have operated as licensed distilleries include: Ballygrant (1818-21), Freeport (c 1847), Glenavullen (1827-32), Octovullin (1816-19) and Upper Cragabus (c 1841). Appendix three on page 144 shows that prior to the Small Stills Act of 1816, numerous Islay localities were subject to the interest of the Collector of Excise and while active distilling may not have been evident at the time, the trading of whisky and other goods subject to Excise was never far away.

Farm buildings at Tallant, above Bowmore

LIST OF PERSONS CONTRAVENING THE EXCISE ACT, 1801

THE following is reproduced from *The Argyll Courts 3, Justices of the Peace in Argyll*, compiled by WFL Bigwood (*see* Acknowledgements on page iv for details).

An action brought by Angus Campbell, Collector of Excise for Argyll North Collection for contravention of the Excise Acts 1801, resulted in action being raised against 19 people from Jura, 233 from Islay and 11 from Colonsay. All were accused of distilling privately, malting privately, selling spirits without a licence and in one case tea and tobacco without a licence. Fifty-six were assoilzied, the rest were fined, none of them more than £10, the majority £2 or less. Decreet, 17th Feb 1801.

The places marked ° have not been identified with places on a modern map and have been left in their original spelling.

ISLAY

Archibald Adair, Bowmore
Charles Bell, Bun-an-uillt
Donald Bell, Balvogie°
Duncan Bell, Kentraw
Duncan Brown, Tallant
Neil Brown, Tallant
Peter Brown, Tallant
Alexander Calder, Ballivicar
Kathrine Calder, Giol
Donald Calder jun, Ballychatrigan
Donald Cameron, Lochnock°
Kathrine Cameron, Giol
Samuel Cameron, Ballitarsin
Alexander Campbell, Bowmore
Alexander Campbell, Mulreesh
Alexander Campbell, Mulindry
Alexander Campbell, Ranochmore°
Angus Campbell, Laoigan
Angus Campbell, Tallant
Donald Campbell, Kilmeny
Dugald Campbell, Rosekirn°
Duncan Campbell, Portnahaven
Duncan Campbell, Skibo
George Campbell, Laranbay°
Hugh Campbell, Giol
James Campbell, Leorin
John Campbell, Giol
John Campbell, Kilmeny
John Campbell, Laoigan
John Campbell, Mulindry
Malcolm Campbell, Kilmeny
William Campbell, Ballivicar
Angus Carmichael, Neriby
Donald Carmichael, Tighandrom

Dugald Carmichael, Neriby
Duncan Carmichael, Ballachat°
Hugh Carmichael, Tighandrom
William Carrick, Ballygrant
Alexander Currie, Ardroy°
Alexander Currie, Mulreesh
Archibald Currie, Ardroy°
Archibald Currie, Corsapol
Donald Currie, Kilchoman
Duncan Currie, Gartacharra
Hugh Currie, Octovullin
Murdoch Currie, Portinellan
Murdoch Currie, Scarrabus
Neil Currie, Sunderland
Robert Dallas, Kinnabus
John Darrach, Airigh Ghuaidhre
John Darroch, Baile Tharbhach
John Docharty, Kilmeny
George Douglas, Bowmore
Robert Douglas, Bowmore
Dugald Ferguson, Tormisdale
Alexander Fletcher, Sean-ghairt
Alexander Gilchrist, Bowmore
John Gilchrist, Glenmolach°
John Gilchrist, Taycarmakan°
Margaret Gilchrist, Torradale
Angus Gillespie, Corsapol
Archibald, Gillespie, Kentraw
Donald Gillespie, Octomore
Malcolm Gillespie, Kentraw
Archibald Gillies, Skibo
Alexander Graham, Ballachat°
Duncan Graham, Ballachat°
James Graham, Ballachat°

John Graham, Ballachat°
Peter Graham, Ballachat°
Donald Gray, Machrie
Duncan Hunter, Kilaire°
Lachlan Hunter, Glenegedale
Donald Johnston, Neriby
Duncan Johnston, Tallant
Duncan Johnston, Tallant
John Johnston, Lagavulin
John Johnston, Neriby
Ronald Johnston, Ardtalla
Donald Keith, Nosebridge
Hector Kennedy, Trudernish
George Kilpatrick, Bowmore
Godfrey Lamont, Portinellan
Peter Lamont, Portinellan
John Leitch, Kindrochid
John Livingstone, Storakaig
Neil Livingstone, Sanaigbeg
Alexander McAlister, Kilchoman
Donald McAllay, Gartacharra
Angus McAlpine, Kilnave
Duncan McAlpine, Kilnave
Charles McArthur, Sean-ghairt
Donald McArthur, Avenvogie
Donald McArthur, Kilchoman
Hugh McArthur, Stremnishmore
Hugh McArthur, Tockmal
John McArthur, Bowmore
Neil McArthur, Mulreesh
Donald McAulay, Bolsay
Neil McCaffar, Kilchoman
Donald McCallum, Arinaman°
Duncan McCallum, Carnbuie

Duncan McCallum, Gartmain
Duncan McCallum, Sean-ghairt
Neil McCallum, Scarrabus
John McCalman, Gartmain
Alexander McCorr, Nerabus
John McCorr, Skibo
Donald McCravie, Scarasaig°
Angus McCuaig, Cragabus
Angus McCuaig, Giol
Donald McCuaig, Stremnishmore
Duncan McCuaig, Cragabus
Finlay McCuaig, Coillabus
John McCuaig, Balulive
John McCuaig, Glenastle
Peter McCuaig, Cragabus
William McCuaig, Cragabus
Alexander McDiarmaid, Torradale
Alexander McDonald, Gartacharra
Archibald McDonald, Machrie
Duncan McDonald, Octomore
John McDonald, Kindrochid
Alexander McDougall, Esknish
Alexander McDougall, Foreland
Alexander McDougall, Lagavulin
Alexander McDougall, Lagavulin
Alexander McDougall, Tighandrom
Allan McDougall, Grasdale
Allan McDougall, Tighandrom
Archibald McDougall, Cill Bhraenan
Dugald McDougall, Geeskill°
Duncan McDougall, Giol
Duncan McDougall, Torradale
John McDougall, Ballygrant
Ranald McDougall, Kilmeny
Angus McDuffy, Blackrock
Archibald McDuffy, Esknish
Donald McEachan Ballachlaven
Donald McEachan, Bridgend
John McEachan, Sean-ghairt
Neil McEachan, Bridgend
Neil McEachan, Saligo
Peter McEachan, Bridgend
Roger McEachan, Saligo
Ronald McEachan, Kilchiaran
Mary McEwen, Ardnish
William McEwen, Storakaig
Donald McFarlane, Torrabus
Alexander McGilvray, Glendoroch°
John McGilvray, Bowmore
Peter McGilvray, Kelsay
John McGravie, Barr
John McIldeor, Blackrock
Duncan McIlliven, Ballitarsin
Archibald McIntaggart, Giol

Duncan McIntaggart, Bun-an-uillt
Alexander McIntyre, Skerrols
Donald McIntyre, Bowmore
Duncan McIntyre, Gortinlongart
Finlay McIntyre, Ballygrant
John McIntyre, Corrary
John McIntyre, Kilchoman
Margaret McIntyre, Ballygrant
Nicol McIntyre, Machrie
Angus McKay, Leorin
Duncan McKay, Esknish
Hugh McKay, Cill Bhraenan
Duncan McKenzie, Octomore
Donald McKerral, Taycarmakan°
Duncan McKerral, Glenegedale
Archibald McLachlan, Robolls
John McLachlan, Sean-ghairt
Peter McLachlan, Kilmeny
Allan McLean, Blackrock
John McLean, Esknish
Donald McLellan, Ranach°
John McLellan, Kilnave
Finlay McLeod, Aoradh
Donald McLergan, Kentraw
John McLergan, Kentraw
Neil McLergan, Kentraw
Donald McLugas, Leorin
Duncan McLugas, Neriby
James McLugas, Neriby
John McLugas, Corrary
Dugald McMath, Stremnishmore
Alexander McMillan, Cattadale
Donald McMillan, Bowmore
Neil McMillan, Glenavulin
Duncan McMillan, alias Bell Portinellan
Donald McMurphy, Robolls
Alexander McNab, Ballymeanach
Andrew McNab, Ballychatrigan
Archibald McNab, Octomore
Donald McNab, Ballymeanach
Donald McNab, Glenastle
Duncan McNab, Ballychatrigan
James McNab, Cill Bhraenan
John McNab, Giol
John McNab, Cill Bhraenan
Robert McNab, Cill Bhraenan
Donald McNeill, Cladville
Alexander McNiven, Corsapol
Archibald McNiven, Corsapol
Alexander McNiven jun, Corsapol
Archibald McPhaddan, Octomore
James McPhaddan, Bowmore
John McPhaddan, Octomore
Lachlan McPhaddan, Octomore

John McPherson, Carrabus
Alexander McQuilkan, Torradale
Donald McQuilkan, Torradale
John McVastar, Carnduncan
James McVurin, Stremnishmore
Gilbert Reid, Kilaire°
James Reid, Kilaire°
Hector Simpson, Bowmore
Alexander Sinclair, Daill
Duncan Sinclair, Neriby
John Sinclair, Texa
Neil Sinclair, Daill
Angus Smith, Esknish
Archibald Smith, Leorin
John Smith, Leorin
Malcolm Smith, Portinellan
William Smith, Storakaig
John Spence, Skibo
Alexander Taylor, Waulkmill

COLONSAY

Angus Bell, Machrins
Alexander Campbell, Scalasaig
Donald Currie, Kilchattan
Dunca Darroch, Machrins
Archibald McAlister, Machrins
Archibald McEachan, Kilchattan
Donald McLean, Kilchattan
Hector McNeill, Kilchattan

JURA

Donald Brown, Brosdale
Colin Campbell, Kenuachdrach
Sarah Clerk, Feolin
Donald Gillies, Kenuachdrach
John Gray, Craighouse
Malcolm Livingstone, Kenuachdrach
Alexander McDougall Achantarbert
Allan McDougall, Kenuachdrach
Archibald McDougall, Brosdale
Duncan McDougall, Feolin
John McDougall, Brosdale
Duncan McIlriach, Brosdale
John McIlriach, Lagg
John McLarty, Kenuachdrach
Malcolm McMillan, Kenuachdrach
Malcolm McNeill, Kenuachdrach
Archibald Shaw, Knockrome
John Shaw, Kenuachdrach
Thomas Thomson, Taychoran

EARLY 19TH CENTURY ILLICIT DISTILLERS IN KINTYRE

The following names have been culled largely from information contained in the still books of Robert Armour of Campbeltown, 1813-1817 and the accounts book of maltster John Colville, also of Campbeltown, 1817-19 & 1823-26. The location is given first, followed by the OS Landranger map reference and names of the distillers if possible or available. In the case of the Campbeltown stills, there are too many to place on the map and the group of stills is simply indicative of the level of activity.

AMAD (NR707382)
John McNish.

ARNICLE (NR708381)
Charles McMillan.

ARUS (NR682212)
Dugald McTaggart.

AUCHADADUIE (NR690368)
John Taylor.

AUCHNASAVIL (NR790396)
Mary Blair.

ACHAGLASS (NR789559)
Alexander McDugald.

CAMPBELTOWN

BACK STREET (NR719204)
Mrs Clerk, Mrs David Broun,
Mary Wright, Mary Armour.

BOLGAM STREET (NR719204)
Misy McKinlay, Mary McMillan,
Duncan McLean, Gavin
Greenlees, Baby McEacheran,
Widow McKivan, Jean Ferguson,
Mary McKiney, More
McEacheran.

BREWERIE (NR718209)
Florence Galbraith, Blew,
Mrs Tarbert

CORBETT'S CLOSE
(NR719205)
Isobel Sharp, Isobel Dunlop,
Jeny Jermy & Co

DALINROWAN (NR7410499)
John Bieth, John Smith, John
Sillars, Archibald Sillars, James
McLean, Nancy Allan, Peggy
Taylor, Nancy Loinachan.

DALINTOBER (NR721209)
Andrew Smith's wife, Cursty
McCarmig, David Smith & Co

LOCHEND (NR718208)
David Addam, More McCost,
Duncan McTaggart, Bell
Campbell, Big Kill, Jenet Eddum,
Mary McKilup, Jeny McKinlay,
Keat McKinvin, Keat McKeog,
Keat Stewart, Peggy Clark, Jean
McMillan, Mary Blew, Jeny Blew,
Nany Shaw, John McColack, Keat
McKinvin, Keat Campbell, Agness
Shaw, Mary Kelly, Jenet Taylor,
Barbra McTagart, Jenet Rowe,
Mary McDonald, Gilbert Currie's
wife & sister, Betty Currie, Betty
McLean, Jean Graham, Misy
McKinvin, Peggy Cast, Peggy
Langswill, Mrs Quin, Mary
McKillup, Jenet Adam, Peter
McKoag, Peggy King, Ket Kenzie,
Ket McNaught, Donald Tyre.

LONGROW (NR717206)
Archibald McKendrick & wife,
Peggy McKillup, Widow Harvie,
Widow Johnston, Mrs McCalester,
Mrs Thomson, Nancy Armour,
Florence Armour, Isabell
Sheadan, Mrs Kilpatrick, Jean
McKinvin, Bell McLean, Keat
McIsaac, Jean McMillan, Bell

McMillan, David Mitchell, More
McEacheran, Agnes McFatter,
Mrs McGlachan, Mrs McSporran,
Keat Bride, Mrs Ross, Jenet
Mitchell, Bell Dunlop, Florence
Armour.

MILNOW (Mill Knowe)
(NR715209)
John McTaggart, Jenet Metland,
Duncan McTaggart, Mary
McLean, Mary McMillan, Mary
Conlie.

BALLOCHANTUY (NR666322)
Malkom Currie, Duncan Morison,
Niel Currie, Edward Currie, Peter
McSporran, John McKeith.

BALLOCHROY (NR728522)
Johnnie Blue.

BARR (NR683368)
John McAlister, Mary McCallum,
Wm McFater, Angus McMillan,
Flory McTaggart, William
Armour, Donald McLean.

BLARY (NR695371)
Duncan McCallum, Archibald
McFarland, John McFarland,
Rodger McDonald, Neill McNeill

CALLIBURN (NR720255)
James McKinlay & Co

CLACHAN (NR765561)
James Brodie, Duncan Gilchrist,
Donald McCoig (also at Loch
Ciaran) Charles Mertin.

CLOINAGART (NR670342)
Archibald McEachen, Donald McLeod (also at Margmonagach).

COALHILL (NR661193)
Frank McKinvin, John O'May, John Campbell, Margaret McGaichy, Flory McCalister, Archibald Williamson, Nany NcArthur, Mary McKinven, John (Mc)Murphy, Bell McSporran.

CRUBASDALE (NR690406)
Archibald Blair

DALBUIE (NR691139)
James McGill

DARLOCHAN (NR672231)

DRUMLEMBLE (NR661193)
John McInnis.

DRUMORE (NR706221)
Andrew McKinvin, Archibald Downie.

DRUMORE-NA-BODACH (NR674329)
Malkom Currie, Neil Currie, Edward Currie, Duncan Morison.

HIGH FIELD, GIGHA (NR656511)
Angus Smith, Donald Smith.

HIGH PARK (NR695257)
Sandy Heman (Hyndman).

HOMESTON (NR673156)

KERRAFUAR (NR678149)
Robert McGill, Robert Watson.

KILDAVIE, SOUTHEND (NR724106)
John McGlachan, Donald McMillan.

KILKIVAN (NR656204)
Angus McMath, Alexander McNeil, J Taggart, John McNeil, Andrew McNeil, James Hue.

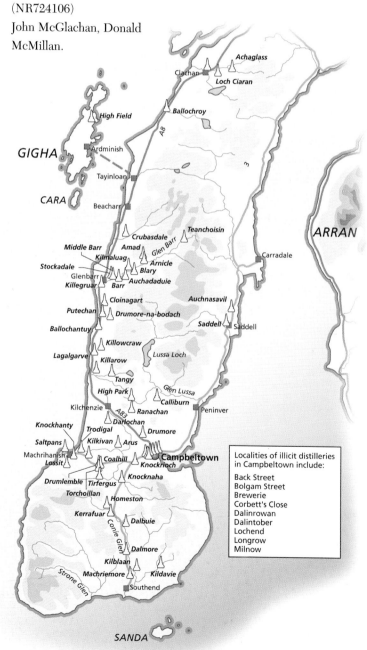

Localities of illicit distilleries in Campbeltown include:

Back Street
Bolgam Street
Brewerie
Corbett's Close
Dalinrowan
Dalintober
Lochend
Longrow
Milnow

KILLAROW (NR662280)
James McMillan, John Blair, Peggy McKay.

KILLBLAUN, SOUTHEND (NR702098)
Hugh Breckenridge, Hugh McEacheran,

KILLEGRUAR (NR667359)
Neill McDonald, John McAlister (also at Barr).

KILLOWCRAW (NR661306)

KILMALUAG (NR693376)

KNOCKHANTY (NR641201)
Flory McTaggart

KNOCKNAHA (NR688180)
Alexander Campbell, John Kelly, Keat Bralachan, Archibald Boid, Alexander Craig, Mrs Craw, James Craw, Alexander McKeith, Archibald McKeith, Malcolm Kelly.

KNOCKRIOCH (NR700195)
Donald Kelly.

LAGALGARVE (NR660297)

LOCH CIARAN, CLACHAN (NR766549)
John McLean, Archibald Milloy, Alexander McKoag, John McKeargan.

LOSSIT (NR634193)
Sandy Cameron, ? Gardener, ? Gardener's widow

MACHRIEMORE (NR694091)
Michael McKilop, William Brown,

MIDDLE BARR (NR677367)
James Kelly, Angus Downey.

PUTECHAN (NR668313)
John McMillan.

RANACHAN (NR696245)
John Maloy.

SADDELL (NR787322)
Alexander McMillan & Co

SALTPANS (NR632208)
Donald Cameron, Dugald McClaverin, Hector Reid (also at Lossit), John Smith.

STOCKADALE (NR678368)
Archibald Gilchrist.

TEANCHOISIN (NR745405)

TANGY (NR674277)
Robert Clerk.

TIRFERGUS (NR662182)
Hector McEacheran, Sandy Munro, Neil McEacheran, Donald McCallum, Alexander Martin.

TORCHOILLAN (NR661190)
Nancy Watson.

TRODIGAL (NR649207)
William Armour, John Hendry, John McKendrick, Donald McTaggart.

Arnicle in Glen Barr, Kintyre. This glen was one of the busiest in the production of illicit whisky in the early 19th century.

THE CLASSIC MALTS CRUISE

The idea behind the first CMC in 1994 was to mark the bicentenary of Oban Distillery. It was organised through the Clyde Cruising Club of Glasgow and the aim was to generate a link between the sailing community and The Classic Malts brand. It would also provide a unique annual event in the sailing calendar that would build brand awareness and attract media attention during the cruise.

The ambience of the cruise was underlined by a loose sailing programme with set meeting points and events at the Diageo distilleries en route. These included ceilidhs, barbecues, nosings and tastings, tours and other activities not normally available to the general public, such as a tour of Port Ellen Maltings. At first all that was required was pre-registration and then arriving on the appointed day (on a yacht!) but the event has grown so dramatically that it is now a much larger animal. In 1995 only 25 boats took part, most of them from Scotland, but by 2001 the number was limited to 100 and the event was over-subscribed. In 2002 the World Cruising Club took over management and the entries showed that 40% of the boats were Scottish, with 20% from outside the UK. In 2003, 39% of the guests were from outside the UK with only nine yachts having previously attended.

Has it worked? On balance the answer has to be yes. When my colleague Chris Marais returned to South Africa after the 2001 CMC, he generated approximately £150,000 worth of PR in articles for in-flight magazines and other leisure and lifestyle publications in his homeland. In the UK alone, the cruise has been featured in all media and has also pumped a lot of Diageo budget spend into some of Scotland's more remote communities.

I have to bang my own drum at this point, because when I chartered the *Alystra* back in 1984 in order to sail around the Hebridean distilleries, I could not understand why others weren't doing it as well. It seemed an entirely logical adventure to me (if there can be such a thing) because a cruise around those waters has everything you could ever want … along with a lot of very good malt whisky!

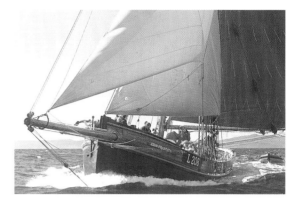

For further info:
World Cruising Club, 120 High Street
Cowes PO31 7AX, UK
Tel. +44 (0)1983 296060
Fax. +44 (0)1983 295959
e-mail: classicmaltscruise@worldcruising.com
www.worldcruising.com/classicmaltscruise

HOW MUCH AND HOW MANY FOR HOW MUCH?

FRANK BIGWOOD explains this thorny problem in *The Argyll Courts* and much of what follows is drawn from his research.

MEASURES

Seventeenth and 18th century Scotland was a place of some inconsistency when it came to how much you got for your money. What is certain is the relative size of measures and liquid volumes. These were:

Grain, cereals	Liquids
4 lippies = 1 peck	4 gills = 1 mutchkin
4 pecks = 1 firlot	2 mutchkins = 1 chopin
4 firlots = 1 boll	2 chopins = 1 pint
	8 pints = 1 gallon

However, these quantities and volumes varied from place to place and in the case of the cereal measures, they were dependent on the type of grain being measured. A boll of wheat, rye or beans in Argyll was equivalent to 167 litres or thereabouts but a boll of oats, barley or malt was around 225 litres which made it larger than the Linlithgow measure, also referred to as the 'standard' measure!

A gallon (nowadays 4.54 litres) equated to around 13.6 litres, which is more than three modern Imperial gallons. A mutchkin was therefore equivalent to a little over 0.42 litres which approximates to about three-quarters of the modern day Imperial pint (0.568 litres).

MONEY

Sterling was gradually taken up by the Scots in the 18th century as they moved away from their own pound which was worth one twelfth of a pound sterling. Sums were often quoted in 'merks' which equated to two thirds of a pound Scots.

So what price whisky and what price malt? On the 13th October 1762, the Inveraray Courts heard a petition brought by Henry Roy Smith against Christian McInnish. As Frank Bigwood records:

The petitioner had sent Christian McInnish to Mrs Shearer for a mutchkin of whisky and had given her half a guinea. She had not returned the change. She said that she had given Mrs Shearer the money believing it to be a sixpence and when she was told that it was not she had gone back and asked for the change. Mrs Shearer said she no longer had it and that she had passed it on as a sixpence. The decision was that the defender should pay 10s plus costs but that she might take action against Mrs Shearer.

From the above it seems that a mutchkin went for around sixpence so a gallon of whisky might have fetched 16 shillings and a pint would have been two shillings.

On the 5th November 1768, the petitioner Catharine McNaught claimed that John McBridan, carter in Campbeltown, owed her 15s 7d as the price of eight pints and a chopin of whisky. That would equate to 1 shilling and 10d for a pint of whisky.

On the 23rd November 1819, the Campbeltown maltster, John Colville sold a boll of malt to Jenny Currie for £2 16s and again on 2nd December two bolls for double the price. In April 1820, a pint of whisky was fetching 3 shillings and 9d. What is clear is that the supply of grain determined the grain prices and they in turn determined the price of whisky.

On the 5th April 1915, the McCuaig sisters of the White Hart Hotel, Port Ellen, took delivery of 35.3 gallons of Lagavulin V.O. for the princely sum of £37 1s 3d! Other factors affected the price as well. Between March 1915 and February 1916, as the Great War raged on mainland Europe, the price of Lagavulin V.O. rose from £1 1s to £1 5s, a rise of 20% in one year.

I looked in at Loch Fyne Whiskies just before completing this book and noted that a 17-year old Ardbeg was retailing for £28.80. That equates to £17.48 for a mutchkin, £69.94 for a Scots pint and £559.54 for the old-fashioned gallon!

BIBLIOGRAPHY

Andrews, Allen *The Whisky Barons*,
Jupiter Books, 1977 & The Angels' Share,
Glasgow, 2002

Barnard, Alfred *The Whisky Distilleries of the United
Kingdom, Harper's Weekly Gazette*, 1887

Barnett, Ratcliffe, *Autumns in Skye, Ross and
Sutherland*, John Grant, 1946

Boswell, James *The Tour to the Hebrides*, second
edition, London, 1785

Brander, Michael *A Guide to Scotch Whisky*,
Johnstone & Bacon, Edinburgh, 1975

Budge, Donald *Jura, An Island of Argyll*, John Smith
& Sons, 1960

Cooper, Derek *Skye*, Routledge and Kegan Paul,
1970

Cooper, Derek and Godwin, Fay *The Whisky Roads
of Scotland*, Jill Norman & Hobhouse, 1982

Craig, H Charles *The Scotch Whisky Industry
Record*, Index Publishing, Dumbarton, 1994

Crick, Bernard *George Orwell, A Life*, Secker &
Warburg, 1980

Daiches, David *Scotch Whisky, Its Past and Present*,
Andrew Deutsch, 1969

Daiches, David *Scotland and the Union*, John Murray,
1977

Donaldson, Gordon *Scottish Historical Documents*,
Scottish Academic Press, 1970

Dunnett, Sir Alistair, *The Canoe Boys*, Neil Wilson
Publishing, Glasgow 1995

Geikie, Sir Archibald *Scottish Reminiscences*,
Maclehose, 1904

Glen, Dr I A *A Maker Of Illicit Stills* Scottish Studies,
vol 14, 1970, pp 67-83

Gordon, Anne Wolrige *Dame Flora*, Hodder &
Stoughton, 1974

Gray, Alan *The Scotch Whisky Industry Review*,
published annually and available by subscription

Haldane, A R B *The Drove Roads of Scotland*, Thos
Nelson & Sons, 1952

Hills, Philip (ed) *Scots on Scotch*, Mainstream,
Edinburgh, 1991

House, Jack *The Spirit of White Horse*, Capricorn
Arts, 1971

Hume, John R *The Industrial Archaeology of
Scotland, The Highlands and Islands*,
(Gen Ed: K Falconer), Batsford, 1977

Johnson, Samuel *A Journey to the Western Islands
of Scotland*, 1994

Knox, John *A tour through the Highlands of Scotland
and the Hebride Isles in 1784*, London, 1787

Laver, James *The House of Haig*, John Haig & Co,
1958

Lockhart, Sir Robert Bruce *Scotch, The Whisky of
Scotland in Fact and Story*, Putnam 1951

MacCulloch, J A *The Misty Isle of Skye*, Aeneas
Mackay, 1931

MacCulloch, John *A description of the Western
Islands of Scotland*, Constable , 1819

Macdonald, Ian *The Largieside Distillers*, Kintyre
Magazine, No 19

Macdonald, Ian *Kintyre Smugglers*, Kintyre
Magazine, No 37

Macdonald, James *General View of the Agriculture
of the Hebrides or Western Isles of Scotland*, 1811

MacGregor, Alasdair Alpin *The Western Isles*, Robert
Hale, 1949

MacLean, Charles *Malt Whisky*, Mitchell Beazley,
1997

MacLean, Charles *Scotch Whisky*, Mitchell Beazley
Pocket Guides, 1998

Magnusson, Magnus *Rum: Nature's Island*, Luath,
Edinburgh, 1997

Martin, Martin *A Description of the Western Islands
of Scotland*, Andrew Bell, London 1703

Maxwell, Gavin *Raven Seek Thy Brother*, Longmans,
Green, 1968

McDougall, John & Smith, Gavin D *Wort, Worms &
Washbacks*, The Angels' Share, Glasgow, 1999

BIBLIOGRAPHY

McPhee, John *The Crofter and the Laird*, Farrar, Strauss & Giroux, 1970

Mercer, John *Hebridean Islands, Colonsay, Gigha, Jura*, Lealt Press 1982

Miller, Hugh *The Cruise of the Betsey*, William Nimmo, 1870

Mitchell, Joseph *Reminiscences of my life in the Highlands*, 1833, rprt, David & Charles, 1971

Morewood, Samuel *A Philosophical and Statistical History of the Inventions and Customs of Ancient and Modern Nations in the Manufacture and Use of Inebriating Liquors*, Dublin, 1838

Morrice, Philip *The Schweppes Guide to Scotch*, Alphabooks, 1983

Moss, M & Hume, John R *The Making of Scotch Whisky*, James & James, 1981 & Canongate, Edinburgh, 2000

Nown, Graham *Laphroaig – No Half Measures*, D Johnston & Co, Dumbarton, 1997

Pennant, Thomas *A Tour of Scotland and Voyage to the Hebrides 1772*, 1774

Pyke, Magnus *Science and Scotch Whisky*, The Distillers Company plc

Ramsay, Freda *John Ramsay of Kildalton*, Peter Martin, Toronto, 1970

The Scotch Whisky Association, *Scotch Whisky: Questions and Answers*

Schobert, Walter *The Whisk(e)y Treasury*, The Angels' Share, Glasgow, 2002

Sillett, S W *Illicit Scotch*, Beaver, 1965

Simpson, W Douglas *The Ancient Stones of Scotland*, Robert Hale, 1968

Sinclair, Sir John *The Statistical Account of Scotland drawn up from the communications of the ministers of the different parishes*, 1794, vol XX

Smith, Gavin D *A to Z of Whisky*, Neil Wilson Publishing, Glasgow, 1997

Smith, Gavin D *The Secret Still*, Birlinn, Edinburgh, 2002

Spiller, Brian *DCL Distillery Histories Series*, 1981

The Ileach, Islay and Jura's local newspaper, published fortnightly

The Statistical Account of Scotland, 1845, vol VII, XVI

The Stent Book and Acts of the Bailliary of Islay, 1718-1843, 1890

Storrie, Margaret C *Islay, Biography of an Island*, Oa Press, 1981, 1997

Townsend, Brian *Scotch Missed*, The Angels' Share, Glasgow, 1997

Weir, Ronald *The History of The Distillers Company*, 1877-1939, Clarendon, 1995

Whisky Magazine, Paragraph Publishing, Norwich, published every two months since November 1998

Wilson, Neil *Ardbeg – Jewel of Islay*, The Angels' Share, Glasgow, 2000

Wilson, Neil *The Malt Whisky Cellar Book*, Neil Wilson Publishing, Glasgow, 1999

Wilson, Ross *Scotch Made Easy*, Hutchinson, 1959

Wilson, Ross *Scotch, The Formative Years*, Constable, London, 1970

INDEX